Escaping Nightmares.....Living Dreams

By
Panther Ajak Mayen

Panther A.M. Publishing Ltd.

Dedication

I dedicate my story to my parents and all those who were there for me when I was in need. It is a dream come true.

All proceeds for the sale of this book will go to the school children of Southern Sudan.

If you would like to help by making a donation, go to:

www.southernsudanschools.org

Acknowledgements

I would like to thanks my Cousin Mawut N. Ajak, my American family and my many friends for their support for I could not have completed this book without them. In particular, David and Florence Reed who encouraged me and helped me publish my story. People like them, like Mike who gave me his coat, Gwen Blackburn who bought me clothes and David Chanoff, his wife Lissu and their son Sasha as well as other representatives of Catholic Charities are the ones who make America, *my America*, the greatest nation on earth.

Forward

Newspapers and television programs were calling them the "Lost Boys of Sudan." They were youngsters who had been orphaned in childhood by the Sudanese civil war and who had trekked by themselves across East Africa. They had fled from their homes as children, some as young as four or five, others nine or ten. As many as 20,000, nobody really knew the numbers started out. At first they found refuge in Ethiopia; then when revolution came to Addis Ababa, they were driven from their camps with great loss of life before eventually finding their way to the United Nations safe haven in Kenya's Kakuma refugee camp. Six thousand or so had been living there since 1992; some were girls, but most were boys (hence "The Lost Boys"). Approximately 3,800 were later admitted to the United States. Most were Dinkas, from South Sudan's largest tribe, but there were also Acholi, Shilluk, Nuer, and others. About 170 of them were bound for Boston.

Until coming to the United States, the young Sudanese men had never ridden in a car, switched on an electric light, watched a television, or used a flush toilet. As children they had lived in conical grass houses and followed their cattle. As refugees they had slept in mud huts, subsisting on a daily bowl of corn porridge.

This is the story of how one of a historically unique group of young Africans, their minds formed and conditioned by the age-old patterns of life on the Upper Nile savanna, is transforming himself and being transformed in 21st-century America.

David Chanoff

Founding Board Member, South Sudanese Enrichment for Families
Founding Board Member, RefugePoint.

Preface

It is hard to imagine the extent of misery that mankind all too often delivers unto itself. Panther Ajak Mayen was only two years old when the shooting began around him in his village in southern Sudan.

He eventually had to flee for his life, leaving everything behind that was dear to him, including his family.

At such an early age he was condemned to running from the war in Sudan to Ethiopia only to find himself fleeing another civil war once again.

In all, he walked over a thousand miles in bare feet. At seven years of age he faced the horror of having to bury one of his friends. The memories were intense, haunting and permanently traumatizing.

It was his strong belief in God that saw him through it all. After many years he was able to turn his desperate situation into promise and success, coming to America where he began a new life.

Guided still by his strong faith, he has been successful in his endeavors in the medical field and was eventually able to return to his native land to search for his family.

Read now the inspiring story of one of the thousands of "Lost Boys of Sudan" and admire the accomplishments of a young man who against all odds, made his life whole again.

About Panther

By

Gwen Blackburn

Radio WXKS Talk Show Host

I met Panther during an interview on my radio talk show. He was an amazing person as were the other Lost Boys of Sudan who also came for that interview.

I would later take Panther shopping to get him some clothes. We went to the North Shore Mall. He was so amazed at all the stores. I got him a warm coat. While driving there, he questioned me about how you can learn to drive, and he also wanted to know about the snow. I thought it would help him and his friends to learn English if they had a television. So, I also bought them a small tv. The young men needed furniture in their apartment so I bought new kitchen furniture, and gave them the table and chairs I had.

Panther began calling me Mom, and I referred to him as my son. Panther wanted to get an education and eventually arranged to go to UMass Boston, where he got his degree. Later he saved his money so he could go home to find his parents knowing it might be difficult to find them after so many years. But with some help, he did find them. It was a wonderful time for him after all he had been through. He called me when he returned to tell me about it and to show me pictures.

Panther and I are still in touch. He drives now, and he keeps me up on the other boys.

Escaping Nightmares......Living Dreams

A Story of Survival and Promise
of one of
"The Lost Boys of Sudan""

An Autobiography
By
Panther Ajak Mayen

CONTENTS

CONTENTS cont'd

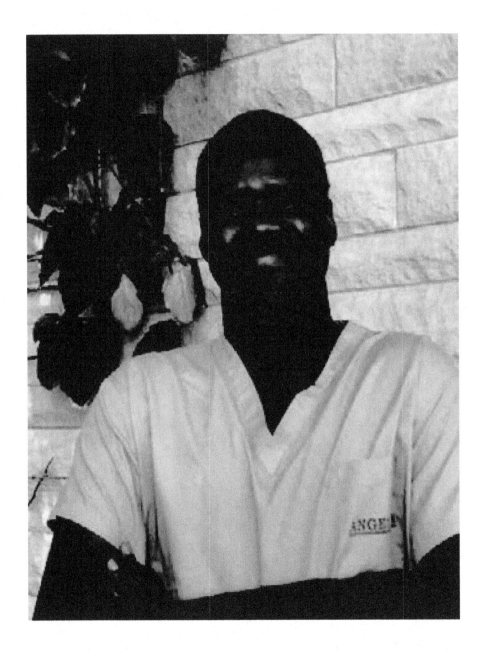

Panther Ajak Mayen

2017

Chapter 1. The Beginning

My name is Panther Ajak Mayen. I was born in south Sudan on January 1, 1981 in the Bor district of Kolnyang village. My father's name is Ajak Mayen and my mother's name is Aluel Yuot. They were farmers and cattle herders in Sudan before the war started in 1983.

I was two years old when the battle began in Bor town. My father had moved our family from the village of Kolnyang to Bor town where he worked as a police officer in the Department of Correctional Facilities. Life was normal in those days. My brother Deng was ten years old, and my sister Awour, was fourteen years old. They went to school in Kolnyang but it was not as good as the school in Bor town.

People were just recovering from Anya 1, the first war. This was the name of the first movement in which a peace accord with the government of Sudan was signed in 1972. That agreement stated that there would be a referendum in twelve years that would allow the southerners to decide whether they would vote for independence or vote for the unity of the country. But before the interim period ended, the government of Sudan broke the peace agreement and dissolved the government of South Sudan. They started imposing Sharia law on the non-Muslims in the south and declared Islam as the only religion in the country.

This was the beginning of the second war in Sudan. The former rebels who were integrated into the Sudanese army started protesting against the rules made by the Sudanese president. The South Sudan soldiers began to plan an internal revolutionary war in the south and other parts of the country where the majority of the soldiers were southerners.

The news of this leaked out and the government decided to relocate the soldiers from the south to the northern part. The soldiers from the south refused to go to the north because the government had broken the peace agreement. After that, President Nimeiry, realizing that the soldiers were not complying with his order, sent two high-ranking military generals from the south to convince the soldiers to accept their relocation to the north. But the generals were part of the internal revolutionary war. John Garang and Kerubino

Kanyin Bol became the group leaders and did not return to Khrotuom to report to the president about the details of the situation in the south. At that time tensions were very high in Bor town between the soldiers of the south and northern part. On May 16, 1983 hell broke loose in Bor town.

The regime in the northern part of Sudan sent troops to disarm the southern soldiers who had refused orders to relocate. War broke out in Bor Town in the middle of night. Our father was not home at that time, as he was at the headquarters of the soldiers who had refused orders to relocate to the north. I was asleep in my room when my mother's screams woke me and I heard intense sounds of gunfire in the city. My mother gripped me by the hand and we ran together to the forest to escape the fighting. As we ran I looked for my brother and sisters, frightened that I would never see them again. As my mother could not hold all of our hands at the same time, my brother and sister ran in a panic to our Uncle Kohl's house. When I heard they were safe with my uncle's family I wept with relief.

The fighting continued for two days until the government of

Sudan defeated the southern soldiers and they left Sudan for Ethiopia for military training. Many people were killed and the Arab militia in the town abducted many children. After we heard the news that the Arab militia had captured the town, my parents decided that we would move to Kolnyang village because the Arab militia would kill those who returned to the town. We lost everything we had but we thanked God we were alive and together. When we moved to the village, life was very hard because we were not used to that kind of life.

Village life was backward in terms of development, compared to the life we had in the city. If someone became sick in the village, that person might die because of the lack of medicine and medical facilities. But in the city, there were many medical centers that a person could be taken to. Also the water was contaminated and there were no roads or markets to buy groceries. Most of the villagers were poor and they worked hard to feed their families, as did my parents. They spent long hours cultivating crops in the gardens of our grandparents to keep us alive. Our daily meal was either milk or maize or flour and sorghum meal. There was no other way of providing food other than growing your own in the village. The only source of water was from rainfall and the Nile River. Women had to walk a great distance to get water and firewood in the forest. Village life was dependent on agriculture and livestock. As time went by we slowly adjusted to village life. My brother and I went to the cattle camp to take care of our livestock and my sisters remained with my mother to help her with domestic work.

After two years the Arab militia came back and attacked the Malek village on the Nile River because one of the high ranking police officers, Makuei Ayen, was from that village. Though he had left the village a long time ago, the Arab militia went to Malek village to burn the houses and abduct women and children. Our cattle camp was located on the other side of the river but there was no bridge to cross to the other side. When they fired heavy artillery and dropped bombs into our cattle camp, we ran to the swamp area to hide there but the water was full of crocodiles, snakes and mosquitoes. We had no choice but to hide in the swamp area until midnight when the Arab militia left the village. The whole village was burned to ashes and many people were killed and displaced. As soon as the Arab militia left the village, we came back to the camp to check on the people who were caught in the cross fire. We were devastated to learn that some of our neighbors had been killed and their children had been taken by the Arab militia. Our cattle were also killed and some were driven away by the Arab troops.

It was a chaotic scene. I was scared and traumatized by that attack. There were dead bodies everywhere and my best friend was killed in that village. I lost hope about the future, because the war would continue for a long time if the Arab militia kept coming to the village and killing more people. Then, living in Sudan would not be an option for me. After the attack, our elders told us that we had to move far away from this village because it was very close to the highway that links Bor and Juba towns, where the SPLA (Sudan People's Liberation Army) rebels and the government troops fought on the daily basis.

In those days life was very difficult for the children who

lost their parents and people who lost their loved ones in that senseless killing. We were too young to understand the nature of war and why the Arab militia was attacking us in our village, as we were Sudanese. After a few months though, we realized that the Arabs wanted to take our land and impose their religion on us. Our elders resisted that change. They gathered young men and instructed them that their land was going to be taken away by the Arabs if you don't fight them. We will be homeless in our own country, and Arab immigrants who come from Middle East, will take the land of our ancestors. The youth took the message from the elders seriously.

Sudan Peoples' Liberation Movement

The young men joined the former soldiers who rejected their relocation to the northern part of Ethiopia for military training. The news spread all over Sudan that southern Sudan had formed the Movement called Sudan People's Liberation Movement (SPLM). They formed the Sudan People's Liberation Army (SPLA) to fight the government of Sudan, because Nimeiry Government was dishonest. The Addis Ababa peace agreement marginalized people in the south and imposed Islam as the only religion in the country. The majority of people in the south were Christian and some were practicing traditional religion. When the government learned that the southerners were flocking to Ethiopia by the thousands, the government of Nimeiry intensified their offensive and attacks against the civilians in southern Sudan. By then there were a few soldiers who finished their military training in Ethiopia and they came back to Sudan to fight the government of Sudan. When the war spread all over southern Sudan, life was very difficult for civilians because the government had put restrictions on commercial airline flights that were used to bring in goods and food items to the people in southern Sudan.

I spent a few years in the cattle camp, but there was not enough to eat so I moved back to the village in Kolnyang. I thought of going back to the village where my mom, sisters, and grandparents were living, hoping it would be better than life in the cattle camp. But it was the same situation there. They had nothing to eat except wild fruit they gathered during the day and their situation was getting worse every day.

The Arab militia continued their attacks on the villages around the Bor area. In 1987 they burned down Mareng village and displaced thousands of people in that village. The news spread to the others villages that the Arab militia had attacked Mareng village, and that the villagers were forced to leave their homes to find safe places to hide in the forests or jungle. After the Arab militia left the village, the people returned but it was not safe for the children or civilians. Again we were forced to leave our cattle camp and village and head for Ethiopia. Before our departure, the SPLA officer, Koul Manyang, instructed the elders in the village to send their children to Ethiopia for their safety and education because the Arabs would kill the boys and take the girls to use them as sex slaves.

Fleeing Sudan for Ethiopia

I was so excited about going to Ethiopia because I was sure there would be no more suffering; that I would go to school, and our lives would be better. The journey began with my three cousins and my brother. We left our village in 1987 with other children who were escaping the killing in their villages in Sudan. I was six years old at that time. We gathered at a Village called Anyindi at four o'clock. The elders blessed us with traditional rituals by killing a bull and offering prayers before they sent us off in the direction of Ethiopia. We didn't know that we were heading into such a wilderness and unknown places where our ancestors had never been. But we had no option except to continue our journey to Ethiopia.

After one day of trekking we reached Guruuk. There was a local tribe in the area called Murle that was an ally of the government of Sudan. It was a very hostile area. We were so scared when we heard that this tribe would attack us at night, abduct children, and sell them to the other tribes who liked to buy children to expand their population. But the SPLA soldiers who were escorting us told the local tribe if you attack these children your village will be attacked by the SPLA and your leaders will hang. So they did not attack us at that time. We were relieved when they welcomed us with bulls and a dancing ceremony in Pibor. After sunset, we crossed the river and settled on the other side for the night and started cooking our food.

That was the beginning of the realization that we were on our own. A lot of children started crying and wanted to go back to Bor, but their elders encouraged them that there is a better place, "don't worry everything will be OK." The life of desperation hit me very hard because I had never faced this kind of life by myself. Despite this feeling of desperation, going back to Bor was not an option.

We left Pibor in the morning and continued our journey to Okilo. On our way to Okilo we ran out of water, so the elders who were with us told us to take shelter under the trees away from the sun so we would not die of thirst and heat exhaustion. Some even drank their own urine to save their life. When the sun set, we started moving again toward Okilo. We were told there was a river ahead of us and if we just kept walking continuously for two hours we would find it. So the elders encouraged us to keep walking. But when we arrived at that river there was no water, just the mud, which was mixed with the urine of animals. Regardless, I jumped into the mud to moisten my mouth and throat, and cool my body from the heat. I thought, "I'm not going to make it because I have seen a lot of people who were giving up and dying under the trees." My uncle told me that if you give up you would end up like those you have seen dead on the road.

As night fell we kept walking toward Okilo. It was very dark. You could not see anything. I was scared of being attacked by hyenas and lions as the area was full of herds of their favorite meal, the antelope. After two hours of walking we heard the sound of herds of antelope running toward us and we knew there was something chasing them. It was a lioness chasing the antelope. Everybody panicked and ran toward Okilo.

On that particular day, we went through a lot of difficulties but we made it to Okilo exhausted and tired. When we settled in for the night, the rain fell and mosquitoes started to bite us. There was no shelter, nothing. We held on for the night and hoped nothing would happen to us. Many of the children were crying and wanted to go back to the village but it was too risky for anybody to go back to Bor because of the enemy.

We spent one day in Okilo then we proceeded toward Pochala. On our way to Pochala town, we found bones along the side of the road of those who had perished on their way to Ethiopia. I was scared and worried that if I didn't keep up I might end up like those who died on the road. Seeing those bones, encouraged me not to give up on walking to Ethiopia, for even if my body gives up on me, my heart is telling me to keep going. I felt bad for those who lost their life on the way to Ethiopia when they thought leaving Sudan would help them. But the journey of escaping the war ended for many, giving up their life in the jungles of south Sudan. Those who gave up were left behind because they were weak and unable to walk to the Promised Land. They ended up dead on the road because there were no vehicles to transport them to Ethiopia. We walked for two days before we reached Pochala, which was a town on the border of Ethiopia and Sudan. When we arrived at Pochala that evening, the SPLA soldiers who controlled the town, welcomed us and gave us some food items because the little food we had was finished. We spent one day in Pochala, then we left Sudan for Ethiopia.

On our way to Ethiopia we passed through an area controlled by the Anyauk tribe. They were not as bad as the Murle tribe even though there were bad people among the Anyauk tribe as well. But we passed a short distance through their land without any incident. We reached the Ethiopian border in the morning. We were sure our lives would be much better than the lives we had left in Sudan. We would not have to be worried about our security and safety or food. We could follow our dream of going to school. But what we didn't know was, there were no cities. It was an empty land with one rusted building in the middle of the town surrounded by forests or jungles. We were shocked and depressed because that was not what we heard from our elders when they told us going to Ethiopia would change our lives. Their main goal was to save us from being slaughtered by the Arab militia in the village. I thought we would see the light and big buildings in Ethiopia, Pinyudu town.

Pinyudu Refugee Camp

After a long trek from my village we finally made it to Pinyudu around the end of December in 1987. Before we could reach the camp, we had to cross a river which was filled with unknown creatures. The elders and community leaders with us wondered what to do to make sure we were all safely on the other side of the river because there were no boats available. The leaders called us together to determine who could swim and who could not. If you didn't know how to swim, those who could would help you cross. Thank God I knew how to swim, and within minutes a large number of us were on the other side. Once everyone was across the river, we started making our way to the refugee camp.

The scene of Pinyudu town crushed my dream of going to school. I had thought that we would be in nice buildings and would have schools and medical clinics for the sick. But this was not like the village I was raised in. This was just a grassy area with trees and no structures. Due to the cold rainy weather some of us got sick right away. In my mind I could see everything I used to do with friends, my parents, playing at home and working in the cattle camp is what I missed the most.

The Ethiopian Government did give us a few supplies such as food, blankets and mosquito nets. They didn't have any shoes for us, but I had walked barefooted most of my life so not having shoes was no big problem. The real problem was so little food and the lack of medical care including vaccinations for measles, whooping cough and chickenpox.

Pinyudu was a safety zone for children and women who were escaping the war in Sudan. We moved into the middle of town, which was secure and safe for us because lions and hyenas were not a threat to us there. As time went by, the little food we had was gone and we had nothing to eat. We resorted to finding wild fruit in the forest. Some children got lost in the jungles of Ethiopia because the forests were very thick and dark. Some were never found. It was a very depressing situation that we were in. Life was very difficult in those days. In Pinyudu refugee camp, we ate leaves and wild fruit. Many children died of disease and hunger because there was no medicines or food in the area. We spent three months in the Ethiopia Pinyudu camp without food and medicine and survived on leaves and wild fruit.

Finally the UN sent representatives to assess the situation. The government of Sudan had sent the wrong message to the UN and they thought we were the rebels who left Sudan for military training in Ethiopia. When the UN representative came to visit us in Pinyudu camp, they were shocked and overwhelmed by the condition we were in. They took pictures and left for Addis Ababa to present their findings to the UN. Two days later the UN sent us food and medicine and set up a healthcare center and clinic for children who were malnourished. Thousands of children died in the Pinyudu camp because of lack of food and medicine. Our caretaker put us in groups because some of us were not old enough to take care of ourselves. We were placed in groups of up to 12 so that the older boys could take care of the little boys.

The mix of children was from different regions to avoid tribalism and discrimination against each other. So our groups were based on region not on tribes. That first year in Pinyudu was brutal because we were mixed with others who did not speak our Dinka language and we didn't speak their language of Nuer. But some people knew how to speak Arabic which was a common language in Sudan.

We started building our huts with grass, leaves and a few ropes. We made beds from what wood we could find. We divided our duties into who would go into the forest to get grass and wood from trees and who would cook our food. One boy in our group died of diarrhea. We were confused and panicked. The caretaker, told us to take the dead boy to the graveyard, dig a hole and bury him because his body was decomposing. It was heart breaking for one child to bury another. I was traumatized by that incident. But when you are on your own you have to accept the reality that nobody will help you out of this kind of situation. You have to be strong and keep hoping that one day this ordeal will be over. It was November 1987, and our future was hopeless. Children were dying every day in the camp due to disease. Missing our parents affected most of us. The few adults who were with us in Pinyudu camp were overwhelmed, but they did their best to help us. There were thousands of orphaned children in the camp as their parents had been killed by the Arab militia in Sudan.

I was 7 years old at the beginning of 1988, when we started school under the trees. There were no classrooms, pencils, books, chalk or blackboards. The teacher told us to write the alphabet and numbers in the sand or dirt. After I wrote A-B-C-D in the sand, the teacher came to see if I wrote them correctly. He gave me a good mark. For me, life was getting back to normal because I did start the first grade, although under a tree. Soon the UN sent us books, pencils and other school materials. By then I was in the second grade. Our elders had built small huts that we used as classrooms.

Still, I believed God had not given up on me. He protected me from those days in the refugee camp in Ethiopia. We faced a lot of problems there but by the end of 1987 our lives were improving a little because the UNHCR provided more food and medicine and sent an Ethiopian doctor to treat the children. Some of us were suffering from post-traumatic stress disorder or PTSD. Some of the children were admitted to the mental health facility because they were dangerous to themselves and others.

To divert our attention from the bad memories of war, and the miseries of camp life, our caretaker introduced soccer so we could compete and create small victories.

In 1989 the caretakers also introduced boot camps to instill a dossier of discipline and good behavior. We composed songs about the enemy and how the SPLA would destroy the government of Sudan and rebuild our country sending the Arabs back to the Middle East. We spent three months in the boot camp before returning to the camp.

We did not know that there was a war going on between the Ethiopian rebels and the government of Ethiopia. Trouble was brewing again.

War in Ethiopia

We thought we could stay in Ethiopia for a while as long as no one was going to attack us in a refugee camp. We spent four years there, surviving disease, hunger and insecurity. We were children who still needed mothers and fathers to support them. But our parents were not there, so we took care of each other. The older boys took care of the little boys in the camp.

The government of Ethiopia was losing the battle against the rebels in Ethiopia so the rebels interrupted our life once again. It was 1991 and I was then 10 years old. That year the Ethiopian government of Mengistu Haile Mariam which had welcomed us to the country, was overthrown by the rebels. Soon news reached the camp that the rebels would also attack us. In the 1980s, the Sudan People's

Liberation Army (SPLA) had collaborated with the government of President Mengistu Haile Mariam to chase the Ethiopian rebels out of Sudan. So it was pay back time for the rebels to revenge what had been done to them by the SPLA. The rebels had established their military training camp in Bonga and Bilpam.

Because the memories of war were still lingering in my mind, I was overwhelmed by the news that our refugee camp in Pinyudu might be attacked by the rebels. I had escaped the war in Sudan and had come here to be secure. But now, we are going to have to move back to Sudan where thousands of people were killed and many more displaced by the Arab militia. The Chairman of SPLA, Dr. John Gareng, sent two high-ranking generals, Salva Kiir and Riek Machar, to address the refugees about the downfall of the Mengistu government.

Salva and Riek told the refugees that we would be moved back to Sudan because the new government was now our enemy. If the Ethiopian Militia did attack the refugee camp, thousand of people would be killed. The only option for us was to flee the refugee camp.

We Head Back To Sudan

In June 1991, we were playing football in the schoolyard when we heard the news that the rebels had captured Gambella and Zinic towns. These towns were not far from the Pinyudu refugee camp. The camp caretaker told us to pack our bags with a few items, food and water. I knew another hell was going to happen to us so we didn't wait. We left the refugee camp and headed back to Sudan.

There were a lot of obstacles to face on our way back. Hyenas, and lions would attack people at night and then there were the mosquitoes. The roads were very muddy. It took us five days before we reached Gilo town, which was located near the border of Ethiopia and Sudan. Some people lost their life on the way back, especially those who were ill and unable to continue the journey. I remember there were three boys in our group, that were left in the hospital. They were very sick and unable to walk and there were no vehicles to transport them to Gilo. I think about those boys and wonder what ever happened to them in the refugee camp. Did the local Anyauk tribe take care of them or did they perish in the hospital in the camp?

Gilo

As we settled in for the night in Gilo, we heard that the Ethiopian rebels had indeed moved into Pinyudu refugee camp and chased out those people who were left behind and killed or captured others. I thought they would not follow us to the border of Sudan but I was wrong. After two days, the Ethiopia Militia was on the move to attack Gilo. At that time a lot of people were crossing the river using small canoes or boats to take people to the other side. Others waited for their turn for the boat. Unfortunately, the Ethiopian Militia started shelling the town and gunfire erupted around us. Six mortar shells landed near me killing five children including their mother.

I was confused and disoriented as to which direction I should run. People were screaming and the sound of gunfire was overwhelming. I ran toward Gilo River with others. While we were running a lot people were shot dead by the Ethiopian rebels. As we approached the river, we found more dead bodies. Many people drowned. Some were shot while they were swimming to the other side of river and some were eaten by crocodiles. You could hear their screams and then a crocodile would drag them under the water.

I was scared and shivering. I thought about jumping into the water but the crocodiles were patrolling the riverbank. I decided not to because being shot was better than being eaten alive by a crocodile. I hid in a foxhole to avoid being captured by the Ethiopian rebels. After four hours, the SPLA soldiers, who were fighting the Ethiopia rebels, had withdrawn from Gilo town and walked toward the river. I heard the sound of people talking in 'Dinka' language. I knew they were not Ethiopian Militia. They were soldiers from the SPLA. I came out of the foxhole and ran toward them. One of the soldiers picked me up and said, "You are a lucky kid." I walked with them toward the south along Gilo River where they used a rope to cross the river.

Pochala

I felt safe because I had made it to the border of Sudan. As we moved toward Pochala we found more dead bodies that had been hit by mortar shells, which were fired by the

Ethiopian Militia. After two hours of walking we found thousands of refugees on their way to Pochala. Those who were wounded were left behind on the road and hyenas from the jungles of Sudan ate some of them.

It took us four days to reach Pochala. As we arrived, the memories of war were ringing in my mind; how we had escaped the war from Sudan and made our way to Ethiopia. Now we are back to the killing grounds where thousands of people where killed by the Sudanese government in their villages in Sudan.

It didn't take long for the Sudanese government to learn that the refugees were back inside Sudan. It was a big victory for the government of President Omar Hassan Al-Bashire because he believed Pinyudu refugee camps and the Sudan People's Liberation Army rebels were attacking major towns in Sudan from camps in Ethiopia.

At that time, there were more than 100,000 Sudanese refugees in Pochala who escaped the war from Ethiopia and made it back to Sudan. So the Sudanese government sent their Air Force to bomb Pochala town. It was around four o'clock in the evening and I was resting under a tree when the bombs were dropped on the town. Twelve people were killed and forty more were injured. I ran into the bushes to hide with other people. After two days the planes came back and bombed the city again. Nobody was killed this time because people had dug trenches to hide in when the bombs dropped. The Sudanese government targeted Pochala because it was under the control of the Sudan People's Liberation Army. Yet the people there were all civilians. After the UN accused the Sudanese government of bombing the refugees in Pochala camp, they stopped bombing the town. It was July in 1991, and they moved on to their next plan to capture Pochala from the rebels, by moving their troops from Sudan to Ethiopia.

Life was very difficult in those days, the little food we had was finished leaving nothing to eat but leaves, wild fruits, and grass. There were nine in our group between the ages of 8 to 17. We divided the duties. Those who were strong and not malnourished went to the forest to gather the wild fruits, leaves or anything that was edible. One day we found a plant similar to plants we used to eat.

We cut the leaves and brought them to the camp. I started washing the leaves with hot water and put them in the cooking canteen to let them boil for half an hour. I then poured the water out and added more water and let it cook for another half an hour. When it was ready, I called the boys to come and eat. The taste was very bitter and spicy and did not taste like the plant we used to eat. We stopped eating it and called for someone to identify the leaves. At that time two boys started vomiting. When the older boys came to check on what we were eating they told us that it was a poisonous plant. Luckily we didn't eat that much. The older boys spared our lives by identifying that poisonous leaf. It was a desperate situation. When you don't have anything to eat, you have to use your survival skills. So we were surviving on leaves of the trees and wild fruit before the UN delivered food. That was in August 1991 and food items were not enough because the camp was overcrowded. We spent a couple of months without food or medicine.

Finally the UN brought in more food and medicine to the

refugees in Pochala, and life was getting back to normal. We resumed our school under the trees because still, there was no classroom. We were preparing to build a small hut for school when the news came that the Sudanese government was preparing an attack on Pochala town. The SPLA called their soldiers to defend the refugees from the Sudanese government troops. We were scared and traumatized by that news. What would happen to us if they captured the town?

We continued with our daily life and considered that news as propaganda. But we were wrong. They attacked the town. Ethiopian Anyuak Militia carried out the first attack on Pochala at midnight. We were sleeping in our tent and the gunfire woke me up. We were about to run to the forest but it was too dark so we stayed in the center of the camp. At that time we were told by the camp caretaker not to run away from the camp until the SPLA soldiers told us to leave. Anyuak Militia attacked Pochala from the south, north, and west. The SPLA soldiers fought the enemy and defeated them. Some people were killed and some were wounded. At that time I knew we were back on the killing grounds. Our lives were again interrupted by the same enemy that had driven us out of our village in 1987.

We were out of options. We could not go back to Ethiopia or stay in Sudan. The only option for us was to leave Pochala and go to Kapoeta. At that time, the SPLM/ SPLA was split into two groups. Dr. John Garang was the chairman of the SPLM/SPLA and Riek Machar was a zonal commander in the Upper Nile region. Riek formed his Nuer tribal movement and committed summary executions of the soldiers and officers who happen to be Dinka and were in his control area Nassir. Riek wanted to over throw John Garang and take over the movement SPLM. Reik sent his forces to attack the Dinka Bor village because Bor was the hometown of John Garang. They killed thousands of people and took the cattle in the village because they believed destroying Dinka Bor people would weaken Dr. John Gareng's leadership.

After we heard that Riek forces attacked the Dinka Bor village I learned that Riek Machar forces had killed my sister. I was devastated by her death. I cried for two days. I couldn't believe it; the sister I loved was gone just like that. She doesn't know anything about politics, and was killed by greedy Politician Riek Machar.

I felt like my mind was going to erupt like a volcano. I even thought about killing myself. My life was upside down. Losing the sister I loved crushed my world of believing that one day I would finish my school and live like a normal person in my country. I had thought that only the Arab Militia would do that, but Riek Machar was an agent of evil and the Sudanese government. We were not safe in Pochala anymore, now that those whom we had thought would protect us from Arab Militia had turned against us in Sudan.

Our future was dark and hopeless. The opposition SPLA was losing ground against the government of Sudan because of infighting among the rebels in the southern Sudan. The overthrow of President Mengistu of Ethiopia was a big blow to the SPLM/SPLA because they got their military hardware and ammunition from Mengistu government. It was doomsday for the SPLM/SPLA and the civilians in Southern Sudan as the government of Sudan captured town after town. Their plan to capture Pochala was to move troops from Sudan to Ethiopia and capture Pochala from the rebels. The news reached our camp that the Sudanese government was moving their troops to the Ethiopian border.

We didn't wait for the hell to break loose again. We left Pochala and headed to Kapoeta. I was depressed and was sick of running from place to place. I asked myself, why my life was constantly full of sorrow and tragedy. Anywhere I go people were getting killed or displaced. It seemed trouble followed me everywhere. I felt like I was an unlucky child, born at the wrong time when people of Sudan were killing each other. But God was not to give up on me. He had protected me from these tragedies. As we left Pochala we were told by our caretaker that the journey would be very difficult because we would have to walk from 900 to 1,000 miles in our bare feet across the desert to reach Kapoeta town on the border of Kenya.

Chapter 2. Running From Death

Living in Sudan was not safe for the civilians or returnees, as the government of Sudan didn't consider us refugees because we were originally from Sudan. However, the United Nations knew we were refugees, so thousands of us left Pochala immediately and headed to Kapoeta, because the government of Sudan was planning to attack Pochala. We had no choice but to evacuate the area. I didn't wait for a repeat of what had happened to me in Gilo town in Ethiopia when the Ethiopian rebels had attacked us. So I left with thousands of others heading to a safer place.

The journey was very difficult for us. It was summer time and the weather was extremely hot and the temperature had reached 100 degrees F. We traveled at night to avoid getting overheated and dehydrated, as well as avoiding the hostile tribe, the Taposa. They were an ally of the government of President Omar Bashire of Sudan.

On our way from Sudan, we fell behind because one of the boys in our group was sick and we didn't want to leave him. We walked with him but it was getting dark and we could not see anything, even the path we were traveling on. We were tired and decided to rest on the side of the road. The moon and stars were not bright as we fell asleep in the middle of nowhere.

When I woke up I saw something moving toward us. It was a hyena. I woke up the others boys and told them what I had seen. W got up and gripped our walking sticks and formed a circle to fend off the hyena. We screamed at the hyena and it ran away.

Our situation was the consequence of war. If it weren't for the war, we would not have been in the middle of the jungles and forests of southern Sudan without our parents to care for us. So we blamed the Sudanese government and the Arab militia that destroyed our villages and killed our people for no reason. We took off and didn't wait for the sun to rise to the level that the heat would bother us.

We walked for two hours before we reached the river at Obodi village or Anyauk village where thousands of people where resting before they could be moved on to Pakok. I was tired and exhausted when we settled down to cook our food and wash our clothes. The next day we left the area heading to Pakok. As we left we heard over the radio that the government troops were preparing to capture all of the towns that were held by the rebels in southern Sudan. Between the use of a new weapon the government had acquired from China, and a lack of ammunition, manpower, and divisions among the rebels within the SPLM/SPLA, the progress they had made in the southern Sudan was diminished. I knew the Sudanese government would follow us wherever we went because they knew the SPLM/SPLA movement was on the ropes. But the true SPLM/SPLA soldiers, who did not betray the people of southern Sudan, were ready to defend the civilians from the Sudanese troops.

After three days of walking, we reached Pakok. The journey had been difficult because the sick boy in our group could not walk very fast. So we walked at his pace.

Pakok was another area where thousands of refugees who

fled Ethiopia from Dimo town where they were staying. We settled in for a few days before we moved on to Buma town. We headed to Buma but the sick boy's condition was getting worse and his body was giving up on him. We had to help him reach Buma town, where he would get medical attention. We encouraged him to walk and not to give up on himself. It took us one day before we reached Buma. When we arrived I asked the SPLA soldier who was at the outpost to help us take John, the sick boy, to the clinic. The soldier did help us carry him to the clinic where he got medicine for malaria and diarrhea. Sadly, it was too late, and he passed away. We were shocked and devastated by his death. It was very painful to watch John die in our arms. We buried him in Buma.

I was scared and thinking too much about "what if I'm sick on the way to Kapoeta and can't make it to Kapoeta?" I trusted in God and believed that one day He would answer my prayers and find a secure place for the rest of the boys and me. It was a nightmare for us. We couldn't believe that one of our family members was gone just like that. John had been a trooper, a kind person who loved to take care of everybody in our group. We lost a true leader and mentor.

We regrouped and continued on our journey searching for a safe place. We couldn't stay in Sudan. It was not safe for us. As we were about to leave Buma town, we heard that the government of Sudan had attacked Pochala and captured it from the SPLA soldiers, killing people and capturing others who were unable to make the journey in search of safe haven. The next day we left Buma for Khor Agreb where we met with the International Red Cross (IRC). They advised as to what was ahead of us and how we would be going across the desert of Kasserngore. They gave us food items and water, because the little food we had was gone.

We spent one day at Khor Agreb. The next day we left around 7 p.m. headed toward Kapoeta. On the way to Kapoeta, the Red Cross and UN agents dropped food and water and set up medical clinics along the way so that nobody would die of heat exhaustion, malaria, thirst or hunger.

We felt like we were not on our own anymore. The world was monitoring us in the desert. As we crossed the desert, the government of Sudan sent their Air Force to patrol the sky and started bombing Kapoeta, Torit and other towns in the southern Sudan that were held by the SPLA rebels. To avoid being spotted by the Sudanese Air Force we hid in the bushes during the day and walked at night.

At that time I asked myself " Why did God punish us? What had we done to him?" Every time we moved the enemy attacked us. Perhaps we were born at the wrong time when the country was ruled by an evil leader who dictated that Sudan should be ruled by Sharia law or military leaders who believed any conflict should be resolved by confrontation regardless of the consequence of killing civilians in the country. Instead of seeking peaceful resolutions, they would resort to war.

As we approached the desert the wind changed. It blew hot air and was very windy. We walked for four hours arriving at 10 p.m. to a location where the IRC had set up a camp. In Kasserngore, we settled down for a few hours before we moved on. The journey was getting difficult for me as my foot was swelling and my body ached. I couldn't walk like those who were walking with me. At times I fell behind because of my swollen feet, but I didn't give up on myself and made it to the location where the Red Cross had water, food and trucks that would take us to Magose. We filled our containers with water, and climbed into the trucks.

The road was rough and dusty and the trucks had no seats, it was a bumpy ride. We had to stand up and hold on to the side rails of the truck. Though it jolted us up and down, it was better than walking in the desert. Eventually, the IRC got us to Magose town where they set out food and water. I was so glad that we were out of the desert and thought the nightmare was over. But the Taposa militia had been trailing us and followed us to Magose. When we got off the trucks we were so thirsty, we ran to the water tanks to fill our containers. We cooked our food, ate and then settled in for the night.

It was midnight March 19, 1992 when the hostile tribesmen

from Taposa attacked us in Magose. They opened fire on us while we were sleeping, killing five boys and two SPLA soldiers. Dozens of people were wounded. It was a nightmare for us. We were not sure which direction we should run. I just lay down to avoid being hit by the incoming bullets. Fortunately, the SPLA soldiers were there to protect us from those criminals. The soldiers fought back and chased the Taposa militia away. In the morning we buried our brothers who were killed in Magose.

At that point I felt like we were walking in the triangle of death because not a single day in our journey went without losing somebody or a life a long the road. We were walking in a storm of chaos. I recalled when we left Sudan in 1987 we had lost a lot of people on the way to Ethiopia. And again on our way back to Sudan in 1991, we lost thousands of people. Now we are losing people again on our way to Kenya.

The Taposa Militia was an ally of the government of Sudan, even though they were southerners. The government of

Sudan had brainwashed them and turned them against the SPLM/SPLA, who were fighting for the interest of the people of south Sudan. The strategy of the government of Sudan was to divide all the people so they could rule in Sudan. Tribes fought against each other in southern Sudan and their progress was derailed.

After that incident, we packed our bags and food items and headed to Kapoeta. The road was very dangerous and the memories of the attack in Magose were still present in our minds. I was scared and worried about the militia attacking us on the road to Kapoeta. Fortunately the SPLM/ SPLA chairman, Dr. John Garang, sent commander Salva Kiir with troops to escort us from Magose to Kapoeta. We were relieved when we saw the SPLA soldiers patrolling the road but still we were worried that the militia might attack us on the way to Kapoeta.

We left Magose around 6 p.m. and walked for two hours until it was so dark we couldn't see anything on the path we were traveling. Then rain started pouring down with loud thunder, lightening and winds that slowed our movement.

But my spirit was strong and I was still hoping that one day I would find a permanent place to settle down and live like normal kids do in Sudan. We were so quiet nobody was talking except a few babies crying. Nothing their mothers could do other than feed them to keep them quiet. I thought they would give away our location to the enemy but the militia did not attack.

The camp caretaker told us to settle down for a few hours to wait for the rain to stop before we moved on to Kapoeta. The journey was long and difficult. As we approached Kapoeta we met young Taposa men along the road but they didn't do anything because the SPLA soldiers were there to protect us. We arrived in Kapoeta early in the morning at 7 a.m. I was so glad that we made it without any incident, even though I knew Kapoeta would not be our last stop. The government of Sudan was intensifying their offensive to capture all the towns that were under the control of the SPLA.

Kapoeta

As we settled down in Kapoeta, the government of Sudan was intensifying their offensive against the opposition

SPLM/SPLA in southern Sudan, especially in Jonglei state, Eastern Equatoria. But they did not attack the upper Nile region because Riek Machar was their ally. The split in the movement had given the government of Sudan the upper hand to overrun the SPLA in southern Sudan. When the SPLA was unified, the government of Sudan lost the war in southern Sudan.

We rested for a few days before heading to Nairus to let our feet heal from the long walk from Magose to Kapoeta. Nairus town was 25 miles northeast of Kapoeta. I continued to be worried about the dangers of living in Sudan, as the Sudanese warplanes rained down missiles and bombs and Sudanese troops shelled the SPLA stronghold and the civilians there.

How could someone survive in this volatile environment, where bombs are exploding on a daily basis and people are being chased and killed for no reason? Living in Sudan was very scary and worrisome for me but we had no option but to stay in Sudan and hope that one day this war would end and we could go home and live with our parents and forget about the life of a refugee and war. I felt like I was born into a storm of chaos. Since I was born there were so many problems: war, hunger, diseases and famine that I never had a good life in Sudan. That was why we left Sudan for Ethiopia in 1987. The memories of war in 1987 would flash back into my mind and wake me up in the middle of night. I had the bad memories of being back in Sudan and the killing ground, where thousands of people were being massacred by Sudanese troops in their villages. I couldn't sleep because of the nightmares of helicopter gunships attacking us in the village and vultures soaring above us looking for a dead body or a weak person to prey on. I was tormented by memories of walking in the desert and escaping the Ethiopian rebel massacre at Gilo town in Ethiopia. I was so depressed and feeling hopeless because being back in Sudan would still not guarantee my safety or the future. So the chances of surviving in Sudan were very slim. The nature of war and the brutality of the government of Sudan would not spare any civilians in the conflict zone. The main goal of the government of Sudan was to eliminate the non-Muslims or Christians and the African tribes in the southern Sudan or force them to accept Islam. But the people of southern Sudan resisted that idea of "Islamization" for a long time.

So I knew the war would continue because the people of southern Sudan didn't want to be forced into Islam or to be second-class citizens in their own country. We wanted to be treated equally as Sudanese regardless of our culture or religion. I motivated myself not to give up and think too much of what would surely happen to me if I stayed in Sudan, which was not an option for me. I felt like we were a cursed generation of southern Sudan born into chaos. My life was on the road for so many years. Though I had been knocked down many times I got up and kept moving, searching for a better place always believing that one day God would answer my prayers by ending this war. I turned to God as my only protector other than the SPLA, which defended us from the Arab militia.

My life had many roadblocks but I believed that life was not a one-way street. It has multiple streets, and you have to be very careful which one you are going to take. If you run into a roadblock, you have to create a way of getting

out of that situation and survive. When we came to Sudan
from Ethiopia we had nothing to eat but we survived by
eating leaves, wild fruit and other edible fruits before the
UN delivered food and medicine in Pochala. Though the
roads we were traveling were very dangerous, that didn't
prevent us from searching for a better place where we could
settle down or stay. So while my life had been bombarded
with tons of problems, almighty God protected me from
these problems by putting his shield above me. I was an
innocent child but never lost my trust in God to see that I
overcame these obstacles.

I met with those who were displaced in Bor by Riek
Machar forces. There I was to meet up with my older
sister, my uncle and other extended family members. We
hadn't seen each other since the war had separated us in
1987. But that reunion did not last long. I left my sister
with her children in Kapoeta. Transported by the IRC and
the Red Cross, I moved on with the boys to Nairus where
I wanted to go to school. The Toposa tribe in eastern
Equatoria in southern Sudan inhabited Nairus town.

I thought Kapoeta would be our last stop but that was not the case. Before we left Kapoeta, we were told by the caretaker that we would be moved to Nairus because the Sudanese Air Force had started raining down bombs on major towns in the south including Kapoeta. This was followed by ground troops, which captured, Pochala, Pibor, Bor, Pakok and Torit. The SPLA had been swept out of those towns by the government troops. Nairus town however had not yet been bombarded by the Sudanese government. It was a good location for civilians to go and stay. Nairus was very close to the border of Kenya. And in the event that the government of Sudan captured Kapoeta, the civilians could be moved to Kenya.

Nairus

We arrived in Nairus on April 20, 1992. I was ten years old. As we settled down in Nairus and started to rebuild our life, the insecurity started all over again. In Nairus, the local people or Taposa attacked people on a daily basis, even though the chairman of Nairus town had told their elders that "These children are not a threat to your community. They are just schoolchildren. Let them stay here."

We spent three months in Nairus as the fighting continued between the SPLA and the government troops on Torit. After two weeks of heavy fighting, the government troops broke the SPLA defensive line and captured Kapoeta. Thousands of civilians were displaced, some were killed and Taposa militia and the government troops captured others.

As soon as the news of the capture of Kapoeta reached us in Nairus town, I thought of my sister and her children. Are they okay? Did they lose their lives in Kapoeta? The news that Kapoeta had fallen to government forces was very depressing. We were in a panic-attack mood because Kapoeta was not that far away from Nairus. From there the government troops could come at anytime to Nairus. We did not want to take any chances and we knew we had to move to Kenya for security. The government of Sudan would massacre thousands of civilians in Nairus. The leadership of the SPLM/SPLA instructed our caretaker to get us to Kenya, Lokichokio where the government of Sudan could not bomb us. Once in Kenya, International Law would protect us.

It was around four o'clock in the afternoon when the caretaker told us to pack our bags and fill our water containers because nobody knew if we would find water along the way. As the government troops were heading toward Nairus, they were ambushed by SPLA soldiers at Buna and retreated back to Kapoeta. We left Nairus in the middle of the night heading to the Kenyan border.

At that time the memories of those years from 1987 to 1991 came into my mind again. I recalled how I left my village and went to Ethiopia and what I had encountered on the way and yet again on our way back to Sudan. Now we were about to cross another international border and I wondered if the Kenyan government would welcome us or would they turn us back to Sudan. The Kenyan government was not a friend to the SPLA, but we had no option but to cross into Kenya as refugees so that international Law would protect us from being turned back to Sudan.

Lokichokio

As we left Nairus at midnight heading to Kenya, I thought the journey would be long like the other journeys I had taken in the past. I prepared myself for hard days ahead despite the fact that we were very close to the Kenyan border compared to the long journey we took from Sudan to Ethiopia and then back to Sudan. We took a long night walk to the Kenyan border. It was a short but brutal walk. We arrived at the border of Kenya where the Kenyan police had set up a checkpoint, to search for guns and other weapons before they would let the people into their country or Lokichokio town. The policemen checked our bags searching for weapons. They were doing their job so that nobody would be smuggling guns into their country.

That journey took me and the other boys in our group, only one day to go from Nairus to Lokichokio. As we arrived at Lokichokio, the UN agents directed us to the forest and told us that this is where you are going to stay while the UN decides where they are going to eventually move you or if you will stay here.

At the time the future was bleak and hopeless. When you are a refugee you cannot choose where you want to live. You don't have freedom. You have no future, no hope and no happiness. You are told what to do. My life was filled with anger, sadness, and sorrow all at the same time. I never thought about the future because, if I'm kept moving from country to country what was the meaning of life? I felt like my life was worthless. I was sick of being chased around by Sudanese government troops. Their children were in school while we were being chased around for crimes we hadn't committed. We were Sudanese children. What was the point of killing us? When would this chase end?

I felt that the only option for me was to put this horror and sorrow to an end by going back to Sudan to join the SPLA. But I was too young to carry an AK-47 or other weapons used by the SPLA in the battlefield to fight the enemy, However, my age prevented me from joining the SPLA. So I promised myself that when I grew up I would join the SPLA to fight the Arab militia or Sudanese troops, which had chased us out of our country. It didn't take long for the government of Sudan to learn that civilians had crossed into Kenya, so they started bombing the Nairus outpost of the SPLA. But we were out of their reach and happy that they could not bomb us in Kenya.

We settled down in Lokichokio and started clearing the bushes and making tents by using plastic sheets. The memories of living in Ethiopia were still haunting me; how we started in the Pinyudu refugee's camp in 1987; how so many people lost their lives in Pinyudu camp due to lack of medicine and food.

Pinyudu, where we were before, was a forest but we inhabited it by clearing the bushes and building houses or huts. We lived there for a couple of years before the Ethiopian rebels chased us out of Ethiopia. I thought that Lokichokio might be our permanent place. The few months we spent in Lokichokio were better than the months we spent in Ethiopia in 1987 without food and medicine.

The UN finally sent us food and teams of doctors to treat those who were sick. The UN agents were here to help and provide food, water, and medicines to the thousand of refugees who were displaced by the war in Sudan.

Kakuma

In September 1992, the UN decided that living in Lokichokio was too close to the Sudan border where the conflict was on going. The UN's main goal was to get us away from the war zone and within two months we were moved to the Kakuma refugee camp in northwestern Kenya.

Even though the Sudanese Air Force was bombing Nairus, an outpost of the SPLA near Kapoeta, and we were very close to the war zone, International Law prevented the Sudanese Government from bombing us in Lokichokio and prevented the SPLA from recruiting young men into their Army.

As we were about to be moved to Kakuma town, the UN representative called the chairman of the camp and told him that he should first go to Kakuma to inspect the area where we would be resettled. I was very excited when we learned that the UN would be relocated to a new area away from the border of Kenya and Sudan to a place where the Sudanese Air Force could not hit us.

As we prepared for the departure, a convoy of trucks arrived in Lokichokio to transport us to Kakuma. Even though we were assured we were moving to a safe place, I had this strange feeling as if we were prisoners being transported to a maximum-security prison where we would stay for the rest of out lives while awaiting execution.

When we arrived at Kakuma and got down from the trucks, we were "welcomed" by a dust storm. The wind was blowing brown dust and sand into our eyes. It was depressing and overwhelming. How are we going to live in this town where the dust and sand blow from morning until the sunset?

The scene of Kakuma refugee camp was like a prison to me. It seemed like there was no escape. It was depressing. It was dusty, hot, and humid. This was a different experience for us. We had never seen anything like this before. The dust caused eye infections and allergies for some. But it was better than dodging bullets in Sudan and running from Sudanese Air Force bombs.

I was glad that we were out of the war zone and in a safe place in Kenya even though the town and its people or natives were very strange to us. The town was remote and undeveloped and the Turkana people there were nomads who move from place to place in the Turkan district with their animals.

The UN agents took us to our group location. There we would stay until the conflict in Sudan was resolved though no one knew when that would be. We moved into our group locations and started clearing the area by cutting the bush and short trees to allow us to build our houses or huts even though we didn't have the correct materials.

Kakuma was not a healthy environment but we had no option to choose where we would live in Kenya. Kakuma was chosen by the UN agents primarily because it was far away from Sudanese border which prevented the SPLA agents from recruiting young men into their army.

The UNHCR started developing the camp by building roads, food distribution centers, a hospital and clinic, and installing water pipe and taps for the refugees in the camp. We spent six months in Kakuma without proper building materials using plastic sheets to build our tents to be our home for the next six months.

The living conditions in Kakuma were very harsh. We could only take a shower twice a week because of a shortage of water. It took awhile for the UNHCR to build enough water pipes to supply the whole camp with clean water.

When the rebels of Ethiopia drove us out of their country, we came back to Sudan and then had to move again to Kenya. Kenya was very peaceful but we were settled in a "gangland" where Turkan men often robbed people at gunpoint at night. Therefore, there was insecurity in Kakuma refugee camp because the natives of the land, the Turkan people, saw us as invaders. But the insecurity in Kakuma was not as bad as what we had encountered in Sudan and Ethiopia. God was there to protect us from the bandits, so the issue of insecurity was not a big deal for us, but we knew the Turkan would still bother people for sometime.

In the first months of 1993, the Turkan gunmen killed one person in group 21 and took his goats and cows. Even though the UNHCR developed laws to protect the refugees, the police who would have to enforce these laws were Turkans. So in most cases they let the criminals get away with "murder."

The UN distributed food every week and life was better in those days. It helped ease the bad memories of war. I felt that maybe we had found a permanent place where we would not have to be worried about being bombed or chased by the Sudanese troops. Kakuma was a safe haven for us and I felt somewhat like a normal child again. My mind however was still in Sudan and I often thought about my parents, my brother, my sister and her kids and my uncle's families, wondering if they were alive or not. In my mind I believed that the God who had protected me for all these years, would protect them from their dangers as well. As time went by, I tried not to think too much about my family and moved on with my life. At the age of 12, I still needed my parents to care for me and support me, but they were not there.

So I lived like the other kids who had lost their parents during the war in Sudan. We bonded together and formed a family of boys. We took care of each other in the camp. We divided the duties into who would get the firewood, who would cook and who would get the water. Life in Kakuma was a life without hope. I told myself that I had found a better place and life would be better here in Kakuma. But the area was full of problems: insecurity, dust storms, high temperature, poisonous spiders, snakes and scorpions, outbreaks of malaria and other diseases. These hardships were a threat to our life in the camp. However, being a child who was born in wartime and had gone through a lot of problems, I had learned about life and how to take care of myself in those situations. Living in Kakuma refugee camp was better than living in a war zone or Sudan where the government of Sudan dropped bombs on civilians and massacred thousand of people.

As time went by, the UN provided us with building materials. They brought in timbers, both long and short, and markutu or coconut leaf along with plastic sheeting for a roof on our hut. After we got our building materials we built our hut to protect us from the dust storms, the sun and rain. Even though Kakuma was a semi-arid desert environment it started raining. Because our arrival brought rain, the local people believed that we were traveling with our God. That was true because God was our protector. When we were in trouble in Sudan and Ethiopia we devoted ourselves to God.

As time went by, we resumed our school or classes under the trees. Because we didn't know when the UN would build schools or classrooms our caretaker didn't waste any time in getting us schooled. At the time I was in fourth grade. Every morning we would gather under a big tree which we called our classroom and the teacher would teach us. When I looked at that tree, I thought the future was hopeless because you cannot finish your schooling under a tree. But when you are a refugee and have lost your country and have no options, you must wait for UN to provide you with everything you need.

Sometimes it took a while for the UN to fulfill our basic needs, and it was very difficult to take classes under a tree because of dust storms and rain. But as time went by, we got used to it. Being a refugee was not easy. You have to be patient with UN agents, so we spent one year of our schooling under that tree before the UN built schools.

It was 1994, and life was as normal as it could be. The UN distributed books, pencils and other school materials. I was so happy because for the first time I got my exercise, books and pencils. It was the beginning of our education. I took the issue of education seriously. I looked at my education as my "father and mother." When you are educated you can take care of yourself and your family. Nobody can take away your education or knowledge.

School and church were the places I found peace and comfort in the camp. When I was in school or church, I focused on study and praised the Lord even though the absence of my parents still affected me mentally.

Chapter 3. The Life of a Refugee

I had no one to turn to for comfort except other kids or boys who were in need of their parents just as I was. We would play games to pretend like we were normal kids. But we were suffering from psychological problems, anxieties and depression from the loss of loved ones and our missing parents.

These were the factors affecting us in the refugee camp that left us all feeling that the future was hopeless and we were at a dead end. There was no going back to Sudan, as long as the war continued. The only way back to Sudan was to join the SPLA and fight the government of Sudan.

I did not take that idea seriously because I knew how I left Sudan in 1992. But as before, I put that thought on hold, and continued with my life in the refugee camp just like a normal person even though the conditions in the camp were very harsh. I had no bed to sleep on. I slept on a single blanket for a mattress and no pillow. I was suffering from malaria and anemia but I overcame those obstacles by not giving in or being consumed by them.

While life in the Kakuma refugee camp was very difficult and challenging, we continued to act like normal children. We would play football in the evening to escape the stressful life we were in. But I continued with a positive attitude hoping that one day God would rescue me from this hardship situation, wipe the tears of suffering from my eyes and give me another chance to live like a normal person.

It seemed like the problems I had been through would continue forever but I refused to be defeated by these hardships. These problems had taught me about the mysteries of life. Being a refugee is not an easy thing, but it had taught me that there are so many ways I could respond to life. I had to choose peace over violence; joy over anger; and courage over fear so that I could survive in the chaotic situation I was in.

As time went by, life in the camp was getting harder because the UNHCR had resettled other refugees from other countries: Uganda, Ethiopia, Rwanda, Somali and Burundi Congole in the camp. Soon the camp was over populated.   When Sudanese refugees established the Kakuma refugee camp in 1992, it was very easy for the UN agents to deliver food on time because the population was not that big.   But the arrival of new refugees from other countries increased the population and the camp became overcrowded.   That meant that the UN had to reduce the food rations and water in the camp.   Before the new arrivals in the camp, the food was distributed every week.   But now it was distributed only twice a month.

Despite what the UN agents said, we were sure that the increased population had nothing to do with the food reduction.   We knew the UN agents were playing politics with our food.   There were a few UN agents that we thought were working on behalf of our enemy, the government of Sudan.   They used the arrival of new refugees into the camp as a tool to reduce our food ration and basic needs.

The reduction of vegetables, cabbage, potatoes, spinach, dry fish, and white flour greatly affected us.   The UN agent that had cut them told us that the UNICEF world food program had run out of funds.   We could not believe what they were saying, and we protested. But UNICEF implemented the changes anyhow.

The food cuts made our lives even harder in the refugee camp because the food that they had given to us did not last that long. It was always finished before the next food distribution cycle.

Most of the years I spent in the camp, our food was reduced to maize, and bean oil, and there was no other supplement to fulfill our basic nutritional needs. As a result, many of the children and adults were malnourished and we were surviving on only maize and beans.

That was the beginning of more hardship in the camp. A lot of families were struggling to feed their children, yet the little food we got was not enough to feed an entire family.

But I hung on to my promise that I would not give up on myself. I was determined that I would continue with my life, hoping that one day God would answer my prayers and find me a secure place or bring peace to our country so that we could go home and start a life in Sudan.

The UNHCR distributed food twice a month, so if you consumed your food in one week you would go without food for a week. We had no choice but to divide our food in half so that the food would last for two weeks until the next distribution cycle. It was a very stressful life, in that refugee camp. A lot of children were suffering from anemia and malnourishment. Many died because their bodies and their immune system could not fight off the disease. If the body does not get basic nutrients, it will break down.

Somehow I continued with my education and finished middle school in 1995 and moved on to high school in 1997. Life never really improved in those years and many times I went to bed without eating. How can you focus on studying while you are hungry or starving? Despite those difficulties I still woke up every morning with determination and hope, that one day peace will come to our country and we could go home.

I lost my dignity and my independence. I was dependent on the world food program. I could not produce anything. I just waited for handouts and those were not even enough to support life. Life worsened in the refugee camp due to lack of services, food and security. A lot of young men did go back to Sudan to join the SPLA to escape a hell life for them in the camp.

Refugees fought among themselves, tribe against tribe, community against community and nation against nation. People were killed in the camp. This situation forced a lot of young people out of the camp, believing that going back to Sudan to fight the enemy would be better than dying here in Kakuma. "You'd rather die fighting your enemy or kill your enemy before he kills you." That was their slogan.

I did promise myself, that before I would go back to Sudan to join the SPLA, I would finish high school. High school was the only level the UN could afford for the refugees in the camp. Going to college was not a responsibility of the UN. It was up to you to find the money or sponsor for your college. But where would a refugee get the money to pay for his /her college while living on handouts from the world food program? I knew going to college after high school was not going to happen, because the world food program was struggling to fulfill the basic needs as it was. I forgot about the idea of going back to Sudan because the memories of war were still fresh in my mind. I was still traumatized by what had happen to me in the past in Sudan and Ethiopia, so I dismissed the idea of going back to Sudan and continued with my education in the refugee camp.

I Consider Joining The SPLA

When I completed high school in 1999, my education had come to an end. It seemed there was no other option available except to go back to Sudan to join the SPLA. I had finished my high school and I saw myself as mature enough to go to the battlefield to face the enemy in Sudan.

I told the boys I was living with, that I wanted to go to Sudan to join the SPLA as living here in the camp unable to do anything would not help our people in Sudan. They had the same idea, so we discussed how we would sneak out of the camp without being noticed by the UN agents or Kenyan police. There were ten boys that left the camp pretending that we were going to collect firewood.

We walked for an hour before we reached the camp where the SPLA agents were waiting for those who would volunteer to join the SPLA. When we arrived there were many people who had left the camp before us waiting for the truck to arrive to transport them to Sudan. When the truck arrived we climbed in and were heading back to Sudan.

I still had mixed feelings about going back to Sudan, to join the SPLA. I knew the consequence of war. People get killed or hurt but I felt good about taking the risk to help my country and defend the people.

When we arrived at Nairus, it was a ghost town with few soldiers as most of them were around Kapoeta to prevent the enemy or Sudanese troops from attacking the nearby SPLA outpost. As we got out of the truck, the commander who was in charge of the recruitment, led us to a place where we would be screened for military training. We spent two weeks in Nairus town before we were sent to the military training camp in Natiga town in eastern Equatoria in Sudan. As we arrived in Natiga, the commander who was in charge of the military training, John Bol told us that he would do another screening because some of us were too young to join the SPLA.

I was screened out with four other boys that were not fit for the military training because of our ages or physical appearance. I was upset and frustrated at the man who was in charge of the military training. Why did he single me out of our group? I thought I was old enough to be trained and sent to the front lines to fight the enemy. We even begged him to allow us to join the military training but he refused. So we were sent back to Nairus and then back to the refugee camp to stay in school until we reached the level the of maturity they needed. Then we could do real military training and join the SPLA combat troops on the front line in Sudan.

I spent several months in Sudan before returning to Kakuma refugee camp. Though disappointed and depressed, I remained optimistic that I would come back to Sudan in the near future.

As time went by, I realized that the man who was in charge of the military screening had done me a favor by rejecting me. He acted a bit like a father. He knew that war was not a fun game and that children should not be allowed to join the army until he/she reached a full level of understanding of the consequences of war.

When I came back to the refugee camp, the other boys who were in our group wanted to know what happened, and why I came back. I told them that I needed to rest and would talk to them in the morning. I went to bed and in the morning everybody came to my hut to hear why I wasn't in military training. I told them that anybody who looked like me would not be allowed to join the military training program and that the General who was in charge of military training was not accepting any children for soldiers for military training. This particular General was not like the other Generals who would enlist children in their military.

He discouraged those my age not to leave the refugee camp to join the SPLA for they would be sent back just like me. Or worse, they would be accepted and sent to war. I told them to finish high school before deciding what they wanted to do.

We regrouped and moved back into the refugee camp. There was no way I could escape the life of a refugee in Kenya. I crossed my fingers for a miracle to happen to me that would allow me to leave the life of a refugee and move to a better place. I prayed for peace in our country so that we could go home and forget about the life of a refugee.

Time passed, and those who were in the military training in Sudan were mobilized to attack Kapoeta in Eastern Equatoria in Sudan. It was a large mobilization. Thousands of soldiers were sent to Kapoeta to start a series of offensives against the government troops. Nine of the boys who left the refugee camp with me were sent to the front line to join the attack. Before the SPLA could attack, unknown groups leaked the news of the attack to the government of Sudan. So the government troops were aware of what direction the SPLA soldiers would come from and they aimed their heavy artillery in that direction resulting in the killing of many soldiers from the SPLA. Though the SPLA kept fighting around Kapoeta, the government troops defeated them which resulted in many casualties. Three of the young men from our group were killed and five were wounded. It was a big loss for the SPLA as a number of their generals were killed and wounded. So the Commander-in-Chief of the SPLM/SPLA called off the offensive until they figured out what went wrong and who leaked the information.

As time went by, I thought about what General Bol, the man in charge of the military training had actually done for me by sending me back to the refugee camp. Had he not sent me back to the refugee camp I could have been in the battlefield like my three classmates, wounded and killed as they were. General John Bol, who was in charge of military training, knew I was a child who could not be sent to war or enrolled in the military training. He saved my life.

Medical Training

I closed the door on the thought of going back to Sudan for now, and began to think about what I could do to help the people of South Sudan inside the refugee camp. I enrolled in the medical assistant training program, which was run by International Rescue Committee (IRC).

I spent nine months in training and successfully finished the program. I then got a job in the refugee camp hospital in Kakuma, which was run by the IRC. I was assigned to work in the ER or emergency room, to help the doctors and nurses during their busy hours. It was a huge relief for me because I was helping people in the refugee camp. At the time I didn't even care how much the IRC would pay me, as my main goal was to help my people in the camp.

My job was to vaccinate children with polio medicine

and teach the youth about the dangers of STD and HIV in the communities in the camp. It was rewarding for me because when I saw the people I helped and they gave me thanks, it made me feel good about the work I was doing in the camp.

After one month, I received my first paycheck. It was KSH 2000 Kenyan shilling which was equal to $30 US dollars a month. At the time, it was a lot of money. Now I could buy myself clothes, soap and food that the UN did not distribute in the camp. So my life was improved a little bit, but still the life of a refugee was a life without hope and prosperity in the camp.

I continued with my life in Kakuma refugee camp still hoping that peace would come to our country and I could go home and search for my parents and siblings and be a normal person again. After several years had passed, God answered my prayers, and sent Angels to rescue me and other boys from the refugee camp in Kakuma, Kenya.

Chapter 4. Resettlement

After so many years in a refugee camp in the northern part of Kenya, life was completely bleak and hopeless. I went to school every day wearing one pair of flip lops, one pair of shorts, a shirt, and worst of all, only one meal a day. That was typical, not only for me but also for all young children under United Nation care. Kenyans and other foreign UN personnel who worked for the United Nations High Commissioner for Refugees (UNHCR) witnessed this unbelievable suffering. It seemed to me that God kept distancing Himself from us every day. The only source of hope came from elders who encouraged us by saying that, "There is a time for everything." Religious people preached every Sunday, "that we are suffering now but tomorrow will be brighter."

One day after school, while socializing with my schoolmates and friends, I heard what seemed to be a "too good to be true" rumor that was circulating in the camp that there was a resettlement program underway. Resettlement program? What does that mean? Those who were familiar with the program broke it all down for us.

I was excited but also nervous and worried because my parents and siblings were not in the camp with me. I wished they were going to be resettled with me. I prayed that God would let this rumor turn out to be true.

As the days, weeks, and months went by God did answer my prayers. It was 1999 when the United Nations teamed up with the US State Department to help Sudanese children. Both agreed that the only way to help these children was to resettle some of them in America. So the United Nation High Commissioner for Refugees (UNHCR invited a number of American refugee advocates to the Kakuma refugee camp to evaluate the actual condition of these young children at the "Rada Barnen Center". They talked to teachers and some of the students. The American Immigration Service saw first hand what our living conditions were. The UN agreed with the United States that the only way to help was to bring them to a place where they could build a new life. Those below 18 years of age would go to foster care families while the ones who were 18 years old and above would be on their own with the help of resettlement agencies

(Catholic Charities, International Red Cross, etc.) in the Unites States of America. I could believe now that this resettlement program was going to be true. After some months, the United States, through the Citizenship and Immigration Department sent a special team, this time, to interview us. The process went smoothly and most of us were considered for the resettlement. In time, I was interviewed and accepted and my hopes were rekindled. I reflected on some helpful statements from elders on being strong and hopeful. I was convinced that God was about to come closer and answer my prayers and rescue other boys and me and from the refugee camp in Kakuma, Kenya.

Generally, it wasn't a one-day process. The UN had definite criteria for selecting who was qualified to be considered for resettlement. This was done because everyone in the camp wanted to go somewhere else with the help of UNHCR. Qualifying guidelines included the year we came to Kakuma.

When the process started, the UNHCR set a time frame for resettlement to be 1995. I came to Kakuma in 1992, so I was definitely among the first group to be considered among twenty thousand children!

JVA Interview

Once screening was done by the UN staff and the refugee advocates from the United States, the more detailed interview process started and began with the scheduling for "unaccompanied minors." This step was undertaken by the Joint Volunteer Agency (JVA). When Sudanese refugees arrived in Kakuma, Kenya, they were in different zones and within each zone, in various groups. For example, group 1 was in zone three. Group 47 was in zone four and so forth. A group was comprised of 150 to 200 people, so the process took a while. In May, five months later, my name was posted on the main board, and those of us selected for an interview were notified. Knowing for sure I was going to be interviewed, questions came to my mind about what they would ask me? What language will they use? I was told that interpreters would be there to help. What if somebody asked me about my parents and I do not know their whereabouts? What if I told the Immigration personnel that I would like to look for my parents first and to put my interview on hold? The interesting thing was that each one of us was asked for a brief personal biography. Thank God my personal story was very short. When the interview day came, I reported to the main gate of the UNHCR with my refugee identification card, which had my name on it. I did not have a passport or a birth certificate. But all agencies under the UN were aware that most of us did not.

The UNHCR gate was well secured. You could see armed security guards with Kenyan police standing there, very serious, which reminded me of the Arab soldiers who used to attack my village. An immigration agent appeared at the gate with a sheet of paper. She started calling out the names. My name was on that list and we all entered the gate. I felt relieved that I had made it inside the gate. Then a Sudanese woman came from the office and directed me to one of the immigration officers. I got very nervous about the interview but was feeling physically comfortable because of being in an air conditioned building for the first time in my life! My goodness, is this what America will be like when I get there? I was getting excited even before

I was asked to answer my first question. My imagination was running wild about the country that I had never been to.

Mr. Mayen, "Welcome, and please be seated." the immigration officer began. The Sudanese woman translated every question asked. I still remember some of those questions. The immigration officer asked me, "Why did I leave the country? Who attacked my village? Why did those soldiers attack your village? Where are your parents? Have you ever been back to Sudan since you came to Kakuma, Kenya?"

In 45 minutes, the interview was over. I was told to wait for two weeks for a decision. When the woman escorted me outside, she told me not to worry because my answers corresponded with my biography.

Acceptance

Even though the interpreter gave me assurances not to worry and that everything would be fine, I still had doubts. I wanted to know what the letter would say because that is how you know for sure. Some friends had already received their letters from the immigration officer. Most of them passed the interview. A few of them were denied for good and you could feel how hopeless they were. I did not want to be part of that group...no way! Some cases were put on hold for more clarification. You never know until you see the word, "Congratulations" for yourself.

I went home that day not knowing what the message would be. My friends were waiting for me to tell them how the interview went. I couldn't wait to explain how nice but busy the UN compound was. The moment I made it home, everyone surrounded me, even strangers. They were very curious! I had a lot to tell them but I was glad the interview was over!

The time frame to get results back, whether you have been accepted or not, was up to two weeks. This was like waiting for two months! I was so impatient! Just as the second week ended, I decided not to go to work on that day. I went instead to the UN compound with friends. I was very nervous but excited at times upon reflecting on what the translator had told me. There was a little structure outside the UNH gate constructed to provide shade to visitors from the sweltering heat in northern Kenya. That is where we were told to gather. Around 9:00 a.m., a white Toyota van arrived and two immigration officers got out. We surrounded them so closely that they didn't have much room to move.

This is it! I took a deep breath while waiting for my name to be called. Within a few minutes, they called my name and gave me my envelope. I quickly opened it and there I saw an "accepted" stamp on the letter. I would be going to the United States as a result of this resettlement program!

I waited for some friends and almost everybody was accepted. What a big, beautiful exciting day! I went happily back home and told everybody I could that I would be leaving the hell of a refugee camp, soon to rebuild my life from scratch. It was indeed with mixed feelings. But my happiness was most visible. I arrived home and started yelling that I will be missing you all when I leave for resettlement. Everyone I met at that moment knew that I had passed the interview. The next step would be a medical check up. Thank the Almighty that I was very healthy regardless of how skinny I was.

Medical Checks

As soon as we all knew that we had been accepted for resettlement, the IOM (International Organization for Migration) took over. Their staff told us that a medical checkup would be conducted and then we would be transported to Nairobi, Kenya. This was a screening process for tuberculosis, typhoid, and malaria, just to mention a few of the targeted diseases. This medical checkup also included taking a personal weight. I only weighed 140 lbs. There were clinics in the camp but what most doctors did was just give painkillers. No specialists. I never had medical records before and was worried that the IOM might ask for them. It turned out that none of that mattered to them. After my checkup, the IOM gave me the results indicating that I did not have any problem. I would have to bring those records with me on my flight to the United States of America.

Pre-departure Orientation

Resettlement is a long process but everything has an end as the bible says, "A time for everything". We were to be given basic orientation on how life would be in America, This training focused on American culture. One of the IOM staff, a young man by the name of Sasha Chanoff, conducted the three-day cultural orientation. This training focused on different cultures and values. It is obvious that anyone migrating to a country in which culture, tradition and other practices are different from one's own can be expected to go through some kind of adjustment over a period of time and not without difficulties. I was straight out of the camp like everybody else, and had little, if any, knowledge of the societal and economic practices of modern countries. So I found it interesting to know what they were all about.

Immigration experts knew that we had unrealistic and inaccurate expectations of life in America. So the training also reduces anxiety by giving or providing us with a more realistic picture on how life is going to be in America. Some of the topics discussed with us included: how to avoid dealing in drugs, prostitution and gangs and how to drive safely and go about working in America. We were briefed on the importance of obeying American laws; doing your duty and respecting law enforcement; paying your bills on time; getting busy with a job search and how to manage your money wisely. Do not do drugs or hang out with bad people or you will go to jail. Do not drive without a license or under the influence of alcohol or drugs for that will send you to jail.

"Your 'Dinka cultural practice' may conflict with the U.S customs and laws related to domestic violence. You cannot discipline your children the way you do in your culture. In America that would be seen as child abuse and your children would be taken away from you."

We were very confused about the American laws because if you cannot discipline your children then they will not listen to you and may do drugs and other crimes in the US. Those who had children at the time when we were in the orientation class were very worried about the American culture because it would interfere with their cultural norms. On the other hand, they were very excited because their children were moving to a better place.

As soon as I left the orientation center, reality started to kick in. I began to believe I would be leaving this hell of a life for a better life and a place where I could start a new life without worries about being killed or displaced by the wars in Africa. I spent most of my childhood on the run, from country to country. This journey of going to America would be better.

Going through orientation, before my trip to America, was very exciting, but I was also scared and nervous. Going abroad seemed like I was never going to come back home and check on my friends who, unfortunately, would not be going with me. Also, my parents and siblings were not with me. It was a stressful time for me.

However, most elders in the community were encouraging. In the meeting I had with the elders, I was told that the only place where you could rebuild your life was in America. That is where I could finish my secondary education, and go to a university and eventually come back home to help my community in Sudan. This encouragement was echoed by those who were involved in the orientation process. Sasha repeatedly told us the same thing: "That once you get to the United States, the door of opportunity is very wide. You could come back anytime you want to as long as you have your passport."

Flight Notification

I received notification that I would be leaving the refugee camp in one week, and that I should prepare myself for the trip. I was excited about leaving for a better future. On the other hand, I felt sorry for those who were not selected and those who were denied for good. I could see the pain on their faces. It was very hard for them watching us pack our few items or bags for departure. It took a toll on them and me too for we had been together for all those tough years in Sudan, Ethiopia and Kenya.

Now that I was leaving them behind and couldn't help at the moment, I promised them that when I got to the US, I would send some money. I also hoped I might get some of them to America, especially my siblings. We hugged each other and shed some tears of joy and happiness. I was again advised about the importance of education. "Please get that America education and bring it back home to help our people here in Sudan," they all told me.

I was going to take my first ever airplane flight in the morning from Kakuma airstrip to Nairobi. Elders have already gathered in scary numbers! Some started talking to me. "Panther, we know you. You are not like some kids we know. You work hard and you respect others. You never break any law. All we expect is that you don't change...please do the right things when you are in America." I listened to all of them. I picked up important advice and let whatever else I thought was not important , "go with the wind." Every Sudanese who made it to other countries as part of the resettlement program had received pieces of advice from community elders.

Then I left them and headed to the Kakuma airstrip. On the way, I met some friends who did not even know that I was going abroad. I said goodbye to many people until

I reached the airport. This time, I was very worried and almost cried. Where am I going? This is a land that none of my relatives had ever been to. As a child back in the village, the only thing I knew about America were those giant planes flying across Africa. Every plane that crossed over my village was considered an American plane and this is the country I'm going to be in a few days. As soon as I arrived at the airstrip gate, it became even clearer, like day and night. Those friends who accompanied me there were told to move back unless they were flying. I made it to the secure area guarded by Kenyan police. The plane was already waiting for us. The perimeter of the airstrip was surrounded by Sudanese most of who were there just to stare at the plane taking people to Nairobi. The clock was ticking! It was time to leave now.

The IOM staff announced, "Everybody, please wave one more time to your friends before you board the plane because this is it. You are not going to see them for a while until you come back to visit them from America." Then I boarded an airplane for the first time in my life. When we were inside, the pilot announced that everybody

must buckle up. "The plane will take off in 15 minutes."
I did not know what "buckle up" meant. Then a flight
attendant walked down the aisle helping everyone to strap
in. I saw what others were doing and I did exactly the same.
I could hear the plane's engine roaring with a deafening
sound. Then the doors closed, and the pilot said some
words over the speakers and I saw the flight attendants
getting into their seats. The plane's engine became louder
and louder and I could feel my posture changing. My first
flight to America would go through Nairobi, the city I had
heard about for years while in the camp.

Looking out the windows, my fellow passengers started
pointing out roads, huts, lakes, rivers and mountains. I
was scared and did not bother to pay attention to what
those seated by windows were talking about. After one

hour and forty-five minutes in the air, the plane landed at Nairobi airport. The flight attendant opened the doors and we got off from the plane. I was exhausted and dizzy because I had never flown before. My head was spinning. After a few minutes I regained my strength and headed to the bus station where the resettlement agency staff were waiting for us. They took us to the resettlement center were we met other refugees who were waiting for their flights as well. We spent three days at the center, waiting for our flight to America. I had never been to a big city like Nairobi. It was a shining city, like Daimon. At night the streets are lit with lights and a lot of cars are on the road. During the daytime, I was like, "Wow!" If Nairobi city was so beautiful, American cities would be more beautiful.

On the 12th of June, the resettlement agency took us to the airport for departure to America. As soon as we got into the plane, the Pilot announced, "Everybody should buckle up. We will take off in a few minutes." The flight attendant provided information about what we should do in case of an emergency.

At that moment, the reality of it all was really kicking in. I thought about the horrible journeys I had taken on foot where we had lost a lot of people along the way. But this journey was a road to the future. When the plane took off, I closed my eyes and thanked God for answering my prayers and now an Angel was strapped under me, taking me to the Promised Land. A land that my parents had never been to. Now I'm heading to America. After a few hours in the air, the flight attendant started serving food. The food was very strange to us, as we never had those foods in the refugee camp. But now, we were eating these healthy foods. Even though it tasted very funny, that was the beginning of our future. The misery of eating only one meal a day was over.

At 6 a.m, after seven hours in the air, we arrived in London. As we got off the plane we were met by an IOM representative. We spent two hours at the airport before boarding another plane for America. At the time, I was getting tired and the weather was changing. It was getting cold and chilly. My body started aching but that was minor compared to the long journeys I had taken on foot without shoes.

We boarded around 9 a.m. heading for America. The time had changed and I fell asleep because in Africa it was still nighttime. I slept for most of the flight until we arrived at JFK airport. Now it was nighttime in New York, and the City was glowing. It was a beautiful sight.

At that time I knew we had finally arrived in the Promised Land, the land of opportunity. Anything is possible. For when you wrap your mind around it, you can find success in whatever you do. Finally my nightmare was over. This was the beginning of a new chapter in my life even though I don't know what life here will be like. It was a joyful moment for me and my cousins who had traveled with me. We spent one night in a motel in New York before we boarded a plane for Boston. It was a one-hour flight.

We arrived in Boston on June 14, 2001. When we got off the plane, the Catholic Charities agent took us to an apartment in Medford, Massachusetts where the people who came before us were living. This was just a temporary house, where immigrants coming from different countries were accommodated and squeezed into for a period of 3 to 6 months.

Chapter 5. America

When I got to Medford, I couldn't believe that the horrible place I used to live in would remain behind us. Now I was in the land of opportunity where anyone can achieve his or her dreams. The days of living without adequate needs were over. We now could try to forget about the atrocities and the nightmares of war. Even though I did not know how life in America would be, I still had hope that my life would change for the better.

Migrating to the United States is a dream to most people from other countries because America is peaceful and law-abiding immigrants can benefit from opportunities that make one's life more meaningful. However, moving to a country that none of my relatives had ever been to was equally stressful to me. My first concern was the weather. During our cultural orientation in Sudan, Sasha Chanoff (IOM staff), whose parents had volunteered to help us, mentioned how cold the winters can be in America. We did not understand until he brought some ice from the United Nation's compound which was the first time we had ever seen ice other than in pictures. We all saw it and felt it. It was indeed cold and we watched it starting to melt. Having been shown this element of the weather in America, I asked myself: How do people go to work? Where do people get food? What am I going to wear when it gets cold?

What I did not know then was how much the Americans had learned of our story. They heard on the news that a considerable number of young Sudanese, popularly known as "Lost Boys," were being resettled in America. This task was undertaken by a number of agencies like Catholic Charities, the International Committee of the Red Cross (ICRC) and the International Institute of Boston, just to mention a few. Amazingly, some families had even volunteered to take some of us into their homes, especially minors, as foster children.

Less than a week after I had arrived in Boston, MA, a number of volunteers visited us. The first ones to arrive were Nelson and his wife Wendy along with their two children, Nelson Jr. and Kelly. That same week, David Chanoff and his wife Lissu from the Massachusetts

Volunteer Association for Sudanese Refugees, came to our temporary home in Medford, Mass. They brought everything you can imagine with them. More volunteers also came including Ron Moulton and Susan Winship among many others.

The first days in America were full of homesickness. My mind was back at the camp, recalling laughs I used to have with friends. I was also mentally occupied with where my parents, siblings and other family members were and how to get in touch with them.

Transitioning

The next phase was the real transition into American life. Our case manager showed us so many things in the apartment. These included: what to do in case of emergency (example is to call 911), flushing a toilet, turning on/off the lights, and using a stove and controlling heat in the apartment. Some of these details were explained to us during the orientation before we came to America, but most of them were just theory to us. Now we could see and touch them. I thought I had learned a lot during the orientation before coming to the United States, but I realized I wasn't even close. It was a different environment because we had never been exposed to the modern world before. Everything was so new to us, especially electronic devices. As soon as we finished our tour of the apartment, we sat down, ate and chatted a little bit. Regardless of how good things were now, conditions in the Kakuma refugee camp still came into my mind. But it had finally come to an end. God had protected me for all these years and I constantly give thanks and praise to Him for answering my prayers.

I knew God was the one who helped me out of trouble and rescued me from the jaws of death. The memories of war still linger in my mind but being in America dilutes the bad memories of war. Life here would be much better than the life I had in Africa. I had overcome countless odds in my life with faith, hope and determination. I went to bed comfortable in knowing that I was in a secure country where everyone has the opportunity to achieve his/her goals.

I woke up early in the morning and listened to a cassette tape, that was given to me by the elders in the refugee camp. I was homesick and wanted to hear their advice again about America, getting an education and life. Their words would help me prepare myself for the challenges ahead of me. As I finished listening to the tape, my cousin walked into the room and asked me. "What are you doing Panther?" I told him that I was listening to the advice that was given to us by our elders in the refugee camp. We chatted a bit and then went outside, sat down in the parking lot and talked about the future. We had been found. We weren't lost anymore. We made it to the land of opportunity where everything is possible if you set guidelines to follow.

Our first priority was to get an education because education is the only way you can realize success in life wherever you go. Getting that American education would not be easy because English was not our first language and the system of education here is aided by understanding a language different than the system we had in Africa.

This is the beginning of our new life. Coming to America has washed away the tears of suffering and hopelessness. Now I'm not worried about being bombed by the Sudanese warplanes. I'm not worried about my health, food, security or water, because America is a country where the Government takes care of its citizens.

After we finished that discussion about our future here in America, we went back to the apartment for lunch. There were a variety of foods on the table to choose from. Because I had not eaten American food before, it often gave me a stomachache. It took awhile for me to adjust.

I heard from so many people that America was a land of opportunities but they don't just come to you. You have to work hard to achieve them and you have to work hard to earn them. If I didn't work hard I might fail, and the only way to realize these opportunities was with an education. I knew I had to adjust to American culture and ways and get an education. Then I will be successful. Coming to America was a turning point in my life. It has instilled hope and happiness in me and put the suffering and feelings of hopelessness to an end. My future is on the right track.

We spent three months in Medford, MA before the resettlement agents grouped us into families of five and sent those who were young or underage to foster homes here in New England. Those of us who were older or above age were placed together in apartments to maintain the kind of mutual support we had in Africa. We have been like family to each other since we were separated from our parents by war in Sudan. The resettlement agents, especially the Catholic Charities, did their best to support us by providing us with cash assistance, food stamps, and a transportation card.

We moved from Medford to an apartment in Chelsea, MA. David Chanoff and his wife Lissu, made arrangements with the Roca organization in Chelsea to give us space where we could all meet every Friday night. They also brought in speakers to help us adjust.

Nursing Assistant Training

Interestingly, they quickly realized that we were all eager

to go to school. David Chanoff, with other volunteers arranged a trip for us to go to the University of New Hampshire so we could see how Americans keep their cows. Back home, Dinka people's economy is dependent on keeping cows.

We were all surprised by the generosity shown by the many gifts friends and volunteers brought to us. We had clothes, shoes, foods, all kinds of furniture, utensils, beds, mattresses, etc. Even the case managers from the agencies that had sponsored us were amazed. Some volunteers started teaching us English as a second language (ESL). English is still a second language and the system of education is different from the system we had in Africa.

It would now be our responsibility to pay rent and utilities in that apartment. At the time, I was not working but four of my roommates were, so they paid their share of rent while I was still living on cash assistance. The Catholic Charities paid my share for a couple months and placed me into nursing assistant training It was run by the American Red Cross. When I was at the Kakuma refugee camp,

I was working as a medical assistant, but no hospital in America would be willing to hire me with a third world certificate or license.

I finished the nursing assistant training and passed the exam and got my license. I was excited knowing that I could get a job here in Boston and support myself and help my cousins who were still in the Kakuma refugee camp in Kenya.

Getting that nursing assistant license or certificate in a short period of time was a turning point in my life. It made me confident that I could complete my education here in the US.

The Catholic Charities agents stressed that before I could continue with my education, finding a job must be my first priority. On July 15, 2002, I applied for jobs both at Brigham and Women's Hospital (BWH) and Massachusetts General Hospital (MGH). After a few days I was called by BWH for a job interview. Before I went to BWH for the interview, the Catholic Charities staff briefed me on how interviews are conducted here the US. They told me to shake hands firmly and make eye contact so that the person who would be interviewing me would know that I was interested in working for that company.

As I walked into the building for the interview, the secretary I met at the desk told me to take a seat in the waiting room until my name was called because there were a lot of people there waiting for interviews.

While waiting, I recalled what I had been told about shaking hands firmly and keeping eye contact. After a few minutes, the secretary called my name and led me to the room where the interviewer greeted me. He shook my hand and told me to sit down and tell him more about myself.

He asked me a lot of questions about healthcare systems and about patient confidentiality. I was well prepared for the interview. I knew how the hospital kept the patients' information confidential. I felt I had answered all the questions correctly. After the interview was finished, he told me that they would be in touch within two weeks. I thought that that meant I had failed the interview. But after only one week, I got a call from BWH telling me that I was to be hired as a PCA or Patient Care Assistant. I was so excited knowing that I would be working at a great hospital with great nurses and doctors.

Chapter 6. I Begin The American Dream

My first job at Brigham and Women Hospital (BWH) was in the 6th floor oncology unit. I was so happy because it would open more doors in this new chapter of my life. I completed a one week orientation on the responsibilities of a patient care assistant (PCA), hospital policy, how to keep myself safe and keep the patient information confidential. After I finished the orientation, I got my work schedule which started at 3 p.m. and ended at 11:30 pm.

The next day I reported to the nurse in charge on 6B. She introduced me to the staff who were working at that time. I was a little bit nervous but confident about my responsibilities as a PCA. It was a huge turning point in my life knowing that I would be able to support myself and send money to help my cousins and friends whom I had left in the refugee camp in Kenya. When I left the refugee camp, I told them that when I got to the US I would send them some money, because I knew the conditions there were not good. I am so fortunate that I can continue to help them improve their lives.

New England Winter

When I got my first paycheck, I paid my rent and food and left the house for Roxbury Crossing where my bank was located. I wanted to send two hundred dollars to my cousins in Kakuma refugee camp for their consumption. It was a very sunny day so I did not dress well for the weather. I didn't know that the weather could change so quickly even though we were warned about the winter weather in New England. I never experienced cold like that before. The chill and cold went into my bones and my body started shivering. When I got to the bus station, the weather was getting even colder but I kept ignoring it as I waited for the bus. I was so happy when the bus arrived because it was warm inside. I did not know that during the wintertime in New England you have to wear a winter coat and winter clothes to keep you warm even if it is a sunny day.

The bus took me to Haymarket [train station] and then I took the Orange Line (subway) to Roxbury Crossing. I got off at Roxbury Crossing station, then went to my bank to send the money to my cousin Deng in the Kakuma refugee camp.

After I sent the money I boarded the Orange Line train back to Haymarket station to wait for a bus. At the station there were many people waiting for the bus for Chelsea. Everybody was bundled up and well dressed for the weather. I was the only person who was wearing thin clothes.

My body started shivering. I didn't know what to do but wait for the bus to come because it would be warmer inside the bus. An older man who sat next to me introduced himself. He told me his name was Mike and I told him my name is Panther. He asked me why I did not wear a winter coat. I told him that I was new to the country, and didn't realize that the weather could be so brutal or change so quickly.

He offered me his coat and told me, "Next time young man, you have to dress well for the weather regardless if the weather looks sunny or warm as it can change in minutes."

I told him thank you and may God bless you for your help. I took the coat and put it on. I could not believe that a person would offer his coat to a stranger at the bus station. It was unbelievable. He saved me from the freezing temperatures. When the bus arrived, I told him that I will give you back your coat when I get inside the bus because it would be warmer inside the bus but he told me to please keep the coat.

On the bus heading to Chelsea, I was thinking about what that good Samaritan had done for me. People like Mike make this country of America the greatest nation on the planet. American people stand up for the innocent people who are in need of help around the world. I learned my lesson in a hard way and I marked that day down as the best day of my life here in this new environment. I told my cousin what had happen to me on my way to Roxbury and how a good Samaritan had offered me his coat to protect me from freezing temperatures at the bus station. I knew it was God who had protected me in the jungles of Sudan and Ethiopia. He had done it again by offering me this coat to shield me from freezing temperatures. He did in Africa by protecting me from the bombs and again in Sudan from disease, thirst and hungry wild animals. I could have gotten sick with pneumonia if Mike had not offered me his coat. He saved me from that freezing cold. I spent the night thinking about what Mike had done for me.

The next day, on my way to the hospital, an agent at the Catholic Charities called me and told me that there was a Radio talk show host who would like to talk to the "Lost Boys" of Sudan. The agent wanted to know if I would be willing to come to her station. I told the agent I would go if she was willing to hear about the war in Sudan and how we escaped the war. The Catholic Charities also contacted some of the other Lost Boys in Boston. Four of us were selected for the interview.

Gwen Blackburn introduced herself and we introduced ourselves to her. She began the interview by asking us questions about the war in Sudan. "Is it a religious war or one of inequality, or is it just discrimination?" She asked. I told her that the war was very complicated because the Arabs in Northern Sudan wanted to "Islamize" the African tribes in Southern Sudan and impose Sharia law on non-Muslims there. Our people in Sudan refused to be converted to Islam. They rejected the Islamic movement. That is what caused the war in Sudan. It was based on religion and inequality and mistreatment of African tribes in Southern Sudan. Our people do not want to be second class citizens in their own country. We explained to her what had happened to our people in Sudan. It was very brutal and some of us here with you now, lost their loved ones or parents due to war.

After the interview finished, she invited us to her church in Medford to talk to the members of her church about the war in Sudan. The church members could help us to spread the news about the war because most American people were not yet aware of it.

We went to the church on a Sunday to share our life experiences, and describe the war atrocities. Before the pastor started preaching the word of God, he invited us on to the alter and prayed for us. After the church service finished, we went to the reception hall and talked about how we grew up without our parents and learned how to take care of each other in the jungles of Southern Sudan.

When we finished talking to the church members, Gwen asked me if I had a winter coat. I told her this is my winter coat.

She said "That is not a winter coat. I will take you to a store to get you a real winter coat."

She bought me a winter coat and a small TV. I thanked her for helping me. She acted like a mother to me. She did what a mother would do for her son or children.

I continued working at BWH doing what I love to do, helping people. I'm not a Dr., or an RN., but a PCA makes a big difference in patient care. I sometimes share my life experience with patients and family members. I tell them what I went through and how God was my Savior in the jungles of Sudan. I tell them that while problems are a part of life, you do not want to be consumed by them.

They should think about the good life they have with their children, your spouse and family. They should continue with what they love to do and be appreciative for what they have achieved in their life and do not worry about the future. It belongs to God and He will take care of the unknown problems.

As time goes by, the reality of American life has started sinking in. The weather can be brutal and the food and America culture can be very hard to adapt to. But we have done our best to adopt the new culture of the new country we are in. To be a success here in America, you have to assimilate or learn the American way of life.

I smile when I meet new people even though I may not know what their intentions are. I keep that smiling face on all the time to let people know that I'm not a mean person or wish to remain a stranger to them.

Unlike life in a refugee camp, everything in America is done by the clock. Everything I do is based on time. Going to work and doctor appointments have to be on time. I move on with my life to follow my dreams.

Advancing My Education

After two years in America, between working and taking ESL (English as a Second Language) classes, I decided that I would enroll in a Community college then go on to the state university. I went to Bunker Hill Community College for one semester. In 2005 I transferred to the University of Mass (UMass) in Boston. I was admitted into the College of Science and Mathematics. I was so excited, because being accepted into that higher learning institution could change my life for good. Education is an asset that cannot be taken away from you. I knew it would not be easy to achieve my goals in education without hard work. But with determination, I knew I could complete my education that had started under a tree in an African refugee camp.

Now I am in the country where every child has a chance to go to school and achieve his/her dream or education. Here in America, if the children fail in school, it is not because their parents did not provide them with what they needed.

It is because they failed themselves perhaps by hanging out with bad people and not doing their homework or not listening to their parents or not taking the advice they get from their teachers. I was very careful in terms of selecting my friends or people I would hang out with at school or outside of school because I did not want to get lost or fail myself. I wanted to achieve the education that I was struggling to get in Africa. America is the land of opportunity so I use that opportunity to improve my life through education. I have seen a lot of kids drop out of high school here in the US because of poor choices they made by hanging out with bad kids who do drugs and do other kinds of crazy stuff that will not benefit them.

Nobody is born poor or rich. It is upbringing that will make you poor or rich. If your parents or their parents made poor decisions in their lives, it can affect generations. To break a chain of poverty for instance, somebody in the family must be willing, or bold enough to do so through education and solid parenting. When you have children, the future belongs to them. You have to give them what they need to succeed in their lives and to explore the world on their own through education.

You have to have a strategy to deal with problems. I had that conversation with those students at school to let them know that they have everything in front of them: financial aide, the best teachers, a good school and a wealthy country. If they fail, who should they blame? Not their parents or teachers, nor the government. It is themselves. I couldn't believe that one day I would be sitting here in a class full of diverse students but God was on my side. He protected me from war, disease, hunger and other factors that affect people.

Now my future is bright. I can complete my education and return to Sudan to help our people in education and healthcare.

My freshman year at UMass Boston was very hard because English was not my first language. I continually worked with tutors to help me with my homework or assignments to improve my academic standing and grades. I was taking introductory classes and finished that first semester with good grades because of the help I got from the teachers and tutors.

My junior year was not that bad even though I was taking hard subjects in sciences and mathematics. At the end of the semester I did very well because of the commitment I made to myself that there is time for everything. I focused on my education rather than follow unnecessary things that have no value to my life. I kept telling my friends that there is no shortage of beautiful women, so please focus on your education. Later on you will find your sweetheart and settle down with your life. I have seen a lot of students moving from college to college because of their girlfriend/boyfriends because they do not want to lose each other. Make a commitment to yourself to finish your education, then get married and make a life together. That decision will keep you on track and keep you out of trouble.

I spent four years at the University of Massachusetts at the College of Science and Mathematics and graduated in 2009 with a Bachelor of Science in Environmental

Sciences, Earth and Hydrologic Sciences. It was not easy being a full time student and working full time as well to support myself. It took a toll, but I didn't care because I knew that opportunity does not knock twice, so I used it wisely. I learned much from my professors, teachers and my classmates. Now the future belongs to me and I will use my education and skills to help our people in Southern Sudan.

Education is the best gift that one can give themself. Investing in your brain will change your life for the better. I will use my education wisely with my natural wisdom so that I can be very productive in society.

I was emotional and overwhelmed when I got that diploma. On graduation day I thought about my parents and my siblings and wished they could have been there to witness what I had achieved here in America.

After a year, I was able to begin paying back my student loans which I had been granted from the U.S. Department of education. These loans were necessary to cover the cost of my education as financial aid and Pell grants weren't quite enough.

Chapter 7. Peace Comes to Sudan

The military revolution had started in my hometown in 1983. I remember the first shots that rang out a few miles away from our house. I was young, about three. By then, everybody talked about the revolution. I thought it was just like two people fighting and it would eventually end within a few minutes if not hours. But it brutally drug on until in 1987, when it became so dangerous I had to run away for my life and leave my village. I was six years old. I thought I was going to be in the bush for only a few hours until the fighting stopped. But I soon realized, after having walked for some days, that this is really serious. My parents and siblings were not with me. Where are they and when am I going to meet them again? I started crying, not because I went without food and water for a whole day, but because I was worried about the whereabouts of my family and friends.

Going forward, the resettlement program made it seem that it would be impossible to meet them again. Even as late as 2001, when the first group of us arrived in America, few Americans, religious organizations and politicians, knew of the war in Sudan.

During the tough times, religious organizations tried to help their fellow Christians suffering without food or medical supplies. But as soon as the first group of "Lost Boys" landed in America, the whole story was on TV, radio, newspapers, magazines, and even in work places. The United Stated accepted close to four thousand young men and girls who had spent much of their life as refugees in the northern part of Kenya. The kind of pain and suffering we went through finally became known worldwide.

Some politicians, who previously did not know much about the war in Sudan, started thinking of how to bring an end to the suffering of the people in our country. One of the agencies, Catholic Charities, mobilized people and brought them to Washington, D.C. to meet with their respective state representatives. At that time President Bush was in power. He watched and listened to our story. Then President Bush appointed an envoy and sent him to Kenya to start the peace process between the rebels and the government. This was the beginning of hope for all of us. If there is indeed peace, then there will be no more killing, displacement, and destruction of properties. Farmers could go back to their farms. Schools would open and children could go back to school again. The peace process was slow but promising. Some countries tried earlier to encourage peace negotiations but all attempts failed. This time it was going to happen because President Bush's envoy convinced both sides to accept peace. The President of the United States was actively talking to the leaders of both warring parties, convincing them to bring an end to one of the longest civil wars on the continent.

As the peace process was being finalized, Dr. John Garang, the chairman of the Sudan Peoples' Liberation Movement and the Sudan People's Liberation Army, came to the US to congratulate the Lost Boys of Sudan on their victory. Peace in Sudan was achieved in part, because the Lost Boys of Sudan campaigned aggressively against the government of Sudan. Their voices were heard here in the US as they spoke of the atrocities, which were committed by the government of Sudan against civilians in Sudan.

In 2004, Dr. John Garang came to Phoenix, Arizona to brief the Sudanese communities on the peace process. Catholic Charities and other organization representatives organized the trip and met with Dr. John Garang. More than 2,000 people listened to what the chairman of SPLM/SPLA had to say about the peace process. He spoke of how this peace accord would be different than the previous peace agreement, which was signed in 1972 by the government of Sudan and the rebels in South Sudan. That agreement ended up being dishonored by the government of Sudan. The government declared Islam as the only religion in Sudan and declared that Sharia law was the only law, which would rule Sudan. I remember when Dr. Garang walked into the hall where the Lost Boys and other Sudanese people were gathered. We started singing songs about the struggles of the people of South Sudan and the SPLA soldiers who defended civilians in South Sudan during the war. Dr. Garang told us that this new agreement would allow the people of South Sudan to decide their own future. They will either choose separation or unity, but it will be up to the people.

We know Sudan will be divided because no one wants to be a second-class citizen or be enslaved by the Arabs in their our own country. That is why people of south Sudan rebelled against the government of Sudan in 1972 and 1983. Dr. Garang assured us that the SPLM/SPLA would work to bring peace to Sudan and end the suffering of their people.

Some of us had not fired a shot at the Arab or Sudanese soldiers during the war but we helped win the war by campaigning against the government of Sudan here in America and other western countries. The peace would bring people together, especially those who are in the refugee camps. I knew then that I could go back to Sudan to be reunited with my loved ones,whom I had been separated from since 1987.

The peace negotiations started in 2002 and ended in 2005. Celebrations were held within Sudan and around the world by Sudanese people. I personally wished that the fierce war, which had killed almost 3 million people, and displaced a similar number of people, had been known earlier by American people. Peace might have come earlier to my country.

Chapter 8. I'm Not Lost Anymore

US Citizenship

After I made my decision to return to Sudan, I immediately applied for US Citizenship. I was so fortunate to have this opportunity because the United States was the only country that was willing to take in some of the Lost Boys of Sudan. Beginning in 2000 until the Peace Agreement was signed in 2005, the US admitted nearly 4,000 of us.

After I had sent my application for Citizenship, months went by without notification from the United States Citizenship and Immigration Service (USCIS). But I was confident that my application for U.S. citizenship would be accepted. I came here legally and I had submitted all the required documents. I was not worried as the processing of an application can take some time before the USCIS notifies you.

The USCIS finally sent me a letter stating that they had reviewed and approved my application for citizenship. They said they were sending me a booklet on the citizenship exam questions. I was so excited knowing that the United States of America was going to accept me as one of her citizens rather than just being classified as a permanent resident. I would be able to vote and contribute to the country, which accepted me and was giving me the opportunity to live like a normal citizen.

I started reading the booklet and all the many possible questions that could be in the exam. After a few days I was notified by the US Citizenship Center that my exam had been scheduled for August 30, 2006. When I arrived at the center, the security guard screened my bag and checked me in. I went to the room where the test administrator was waiting for me. She introduced herself and asked for my full name and date of birth.

She started the exam by reading me questions:
"Who is the President of the United States? Who was the Governor of Massachusetts? When was the United Nations formed? And who was the President of the United States when it was formed?"

I thought the exam would be a written exam but it was oral.

When she finished reading the exam questions she asked me if I was ready. I told her "yes I'm ready." She read the questions listed above and I answered them correctly. President of the United States is George Bush. The Secretary of State is Condoleezza Rice. The Governor of Massachusetts is Mitt Romney. The United Nations was formed January 1, 1942, and the president of the United States at the time was Franklin Roosevelt.

After I answered those questions, the test administrator told me "congratulations, you have passed your citizenship test. Next, we will send you your swearing-in date." Considering that I had spent most of my childhood in refugee camps or just surviving in the jungles of foreign countries, I was overjoyed about becoming a United States Citizen. The years of being "stateless" were over. Now I had a country where I have the opportunity to live like a normal person.

The days of the Lost Boys were over for me. On June 30, 2007, I was sworn in as a citizen of the United States. It was a joyful day for me.

US Passport

As soon as I got my citizenship, I applied for a US Passport. Now I could go back to Sudan to search for my parents and siblings. Since the peace was signed in 2005, people were moving back to Sudan from neighboring countries. There was no war. The guns were silent. People were moving from region to region to search for missing loved ones that the war had scattered all over Sudan. You didn't know who was alive and who was not. People kept crossing their fingers and praying that they would find their loved ones alive and well.

While I was waiting for my passport, I contacted my cousin in Kenya to ask him if he heard anything about my parents and siblings in Sudan. He told me that he hadn't heard anything about them or where they were, but that he would let me know if he heard anything. "Let's hope for the best," he answered.

While I was processing those feelings, my passport arrived. I was so happy because I never thought one day

I would be holding this American passport in my hands. But with hope and determination I made it to the Promised Land, the land of opportunity and prosperity. Now I can travel anywhere I want around the world without any restrictions.

Chapter 9. Return to Sudan

In December 2008, I got my tickets. I was so excited because I would go back to the land I left, or rather that I was chased out of. I was feeling more certain than ever that I would find my parents and siblings. I was going "home."

At the time, many things came into my mind. What of if I do not find my parents and siblings? How would I know what had happen to them? I was struggling to erase those negative thoughts and I just assumed that they were okay wherever they are.

I continued working for a couple more months to save money for my trip before my departure. I was executed because the war was over and people would be going back to Sudan, especially those who were in the refugee camps or in neighboring countries who could return to rebuild their lives and live like normal people. No longer would they have to worry about being bombed by the Movement or the government of Sudan.

On December 15, 2008, I left for Africa. I was like wow! I couldn't believe that this day had come, that I was going back to Sudan where we had been bombed and killed for no reason. It was a very scary moment for me because I did not trust the government of Sudan. The President of Sudan is an unpredictable man. His words do not match his actions. Thus, this peace might end up like the 1972 peace agreement that the government dishonored.

But I trust almighty God will bring peace to the people of Sudan because they have been suffering for too many years. Some of us, who were born during wartime, knew nothing of a peaceful life in Sudan. The only thing we knew was destruction and killing of innocent people by the government of Sudan. Fortunately, the international community, particularly the United States and church leaders, have put pressure on the warring parties to honor the peace they signed in 2005.

My return to Sudan was full of mixed feelings, but I kept my fingers crossed hoping that I would be home soon and find out what had happen to my relatives in Sudan. I haven't heard from most of my family or relatives and I haven't seen them in 23 years.

At Heathrow, London Airport, I changed to the plane that was going to Nairobi, Kenya. While there, I met two Lost Boys of Sudan whom I had known when we were in the Kakuma refugee camp. They too were going back to Sudan. We chatted a little about life in America and of the peace in Sudan. One of them, named Garang didn't know where his parents were. He was worried that his parents might not be alive because he kept calling his relatives to find out where they were but nobody could give him the answer he wanted to hear. So he decided that the only way to find them was to go to Sudan. I realized that we had the same thought about our parents because I too hadn't heard from my parents for many years. I told him, "Listen Garang, do not think too much about the negativity of what had happen to your parents. I have had the same thoughts but I try to think positive. If no one has called you and said your parents are dead, then believe that they are alive and well wherever they are."

So both of us were going back to Sudan to look for our loved ones, even though our route was not the same. They were going to Uganda, Kampala and I was going to Nairobi, Kenya then on to Juba, South Sudan.

After we had that brief discussion, I said goodbye and boarded the plane for Nairobi. I spent 8 hours on the plane worrying about what the news would be about my parents and siblings because so many people were killed and displaced by the war. As soon as our plane touched down at Jumbo, Kenyatta Airport in Nairobi, I got off the plane and headed to the immigration and customs office to get a visa so I could exit the airport. After I paid for my visa, I went to the luggage area to claim my bag, and then exited the airport. As soon as I went out the door, my cousin Deng was waiting for me. At first I didn't see him because of all the people in the waiting area. Finally I saw him waving his hand at me. I walked right to him and we hugged each other. It was a great reunion. I hadn't seen him in five years, ever since I left the Kakuma refugee camp in 2001. We talked a bit about life in the refugee camp, peace in our country and how we would go about finding the town they were in and how to contact them.

We got into a taxi and headed to his place where I would spend a few days before going home to Sudan to look for my parents and siblings. He said he hadn't heard anything about my family. He had talked to some of our relatives in Sudan, but nobody knew where they were. It was stressful not knowing where they were. I was running out of patience, but my cousin told me we couldn't go to Sudan until we knew what part of Sudan they were in. A lot of people were displaced during the war and people were moving from region to region looking for missing relatives or loved ones. Many were alive and living in the refugee camps, but now that peace has come to our country, everybody was moving freely without worry of being killed.

I decided to travel to Sudan by Friday regardless; even not knowing what region my family might be in. After we finished talking, my uncle called Deng, his son, and told him to let me know that my parents and siblings were alive and well in Bortown in Jonglei state in Sudan. After my cousin finished talking to his Dad, he told me. I almost broke down. I thought they were dead. I was so relieved and happy about the news that they were living in South Sudan. During the war, communications regarding the movement of people from place to place was cut off.

After that phone call from my uncle about my parents and siblings, I bought some clothes and school materials especially books, exercise books, pen, pencils, and chalk for the children in the village school. Before I left the U.S., Gwen Blackburn (the great woman who bought me a winter coat in 2001) and her church members, raised $600 US dollars for my trip so that I could buy school materials that the children in the village school were lacking. It was a huge help from Gwen and the members of her church.

After I purchased these items, I bought my ticket for Sudan and I asked my uncle Buk to inform my brother and sisters that I would be traveling to Juba in two days. One of them would have to take me to Bortown where our parents were. I spent two days with my cousin in Nairobi before I left for Sudan. I was so anxious to get home because it had been 23 years since I left Sudan in 1987. It would be an emotional reunion.

Juba, Sudan

I packed my bag with the school items and headed to the airport where I boarded a Kenyan Airline flight to Juba, Sudan. After an hour in the air, the pilot announced that we would be landing shortly. The dream of one day seeing my family and relatives again was coming true. I never doubted that almighty God, who protected me and my family from the evils of war all these years, would see me through to this day. This was now a time for peace, the silencing of guns and the reunions of families. It's never been quite like this in Sudan before.

Now I'm back to the place I had to run from to save my life. I got off the plane and went to the immigration and customs office to get a visa. I paid the visa fees and exited the airport to meet my brother and sister who were waiting to meet me. I wasn't sure I would recognize them. But I felt sure I would remember their faces even though they were older than me. As soon as I walked into the waiting area, I saw my brother standing next to my sister. I recognized his face and then I called him Deng. He looked at me and asked, "Is that you Panther?"

I ran to them and hugged him, my sisters and cousins. I could not believe that this day had come. Tears of joy and happiness rolled down my cheek. The nightmare had come to an end. There is nothing like the bond between brothers and sisters. Now we were back together. We left the airport heading to my uncle Koul's house. As we arrived, everybody who was in the compound started calling me by my childhood nickname, Luak Anyierdit, which kids used to call me in the cattle camp. Calling me by my nickname refreshed my childhood memories. We sat down under the tree in the compound of Uncle Koul. A lot of people came to greet me and to ask about their children who were in America. I told the relatives of the children who were in America in the State of Massachusetts, that their children were doing well and some of them would surely come to visit if the peace holds. Of those who were in the refugee camp I have no clue because I haven't visited Kakuma refugee camp. I spent the whole night talking with people about life in America and of their life in Sudan in general.

I spent three days in Juba, Sudan with my siblings. Finally it was time to go to Bor where my parents were. It was a three-hour drive to the Bor area. As we approached the town I was getting emotional about returning to the place where hell broke loose in the 1980's. I was almost killed, and had to run for my life. In my mind, it seemed like I was going back to the crime scene where the war broke out. I realized that the flash back of war memories would only ruin my reunions so I shut down those negative thoughts. I turned them into joyful feelings, ever so grateful that I made it back home safely and thankful to almighty God, who protected me all these years.

Malek Village

We drove for another 20 minutes to Malek village, which is located on the banks of the Nile River. We stopped there to greet people and members of our community who were living in Malek. Malek was one of the places that was attacked by Arab militia or government troops in 1987. The village was burned down, cattle and livestock were looted and women and children were abducted. People got killed here in Malek. The memories of war were still fresh in my mind, so I embraced the peace as it will heal the wounds of war and bring the people of Sudan together. As we left Malek village, I saw a lot of people walking on the side of road, heading to Bortown to get some items from the markets in Bortown. I could see on their faces that life was back to normal. Nobody was worried about war anymore.

We arrived in Bortown and went immediately to my brother's house to meet his wife and son, and other relatives who were there in Bortown. We spent two days in Bortown before traveling on to Kolnyang village to see my parents. I was impatient. I couldn't wait anymore and I rented a car to take us to Kolnyang village or Gwalla. The journey was a one-hour drive and we arrived around noon. My Dad and Mom and other relatives were waiting for me at the station where the buses and cars drop people off.

Home

As soon as the car stopped, I got out and ran to meet my parents. I could not believe this day had come. There is nothing like the bond between a mother and father and their children. My mom couldn't stop crying. She could not believe that she would again hold me in her arms like the little boy she used to take care of in the 1980's. My Dad told me that the God of our ancestors had protected me and brought me home safely. It was an emotional reunion and joyful for me and my parents.

After 23 years of separation, almighty God has made it

Aluel Yuot, Ajak Mayen and Panther Mayen

possible for us to be together again as a family. The nightmares and loneliness are over. I'm home. Home sweet home. "The land of honey, wild fruits and milk." There is nothing like home. We were reunited, sitting together as a family and sharing childhood stories with my brother, sisters, cousins and friends. My lost childhood memories needed to be relived. I still remember some of the playing grounds and the games we used to play back in those days. I visited the cattle camp of Ayicrou and Jangakuce that we used for camping and keeping our cattle during the rainy season, before we would take them to the riverbank in the summer. Catching up with my lost childhood memories made me feel like a child again, like I was reborn. God is great. I made it home.

I slept like a baby knowing nothing would happen to me because my parents were there to protect me from danger. The dark days I spent without my parents are now over. The air feels fresh and the land is peaceful.

I spent the whole day talking with my parents of things that I could not remember from when I was a child. After we shared those memories, dinner was ready and we sat around the table as a family, eating together for the first time in over two decades. Seeing my parents and sibling was the beginning of a long healing process.

The next day my Dad called the people in the village to come to our house to pray for me. They brought a bull and two goats for ceremonies and prayer. My sisters and cousins prepared the meal for us. When the meal was ready, the priest blessed the ceremonies. He thanked God for protecting me during the war.

Our lost son is lost no longer.
My dream has come true.

Seeing my parents cleared my mind from the nightmares of war. It was a blessing to see my parents and siblings again, and for the first time in decades sitting together as a big family even though my sister and cousins, uncles who were killed during the war were not present with us physically, spiritually they were with us.

The next day I visited some of my old friends, my "ag-mates" to celebrate my return and talk about our lost childhood memories; how we went to the forest to gather wild fruits and taking our calves or cattle for grazing. I also visited the school to deliver the school supplies to the children. Even though there were not enough supplies for everyone, they were happy and thankful for what they had been given by the American people.

In my entire life, I had never felt that happy. I was comfortable then as now, spiritually, physically and mentality. My life was back to normal. Visiting the place I was born set me free from the traumas of war and the dark lonely days without my parents.

Going home put a big smile on my face and freed me from the Post Traumatic Stress Disorder I was suffering from. It was great therapy for me and my parents because missing your child or your parents for that long is not an easy thing to endure. But my time there had come to an end. I couldn't believe time had gone by so fast and now it was time to travel back to Nairobi, Kenya for my flight back to the US.

My parents later sent me this note about my entire ordeal

To Our Son Panther

Dear son,

You should know that we have been wondering whether you were alive or not for all these years. We sent a number of letters through the Red Cross but never heard back. Some returnees from the Kakuma refugee camp said that you were there and attending school. Everybody was worried about your whereabouts.

We are all thankful that you survived the most hostile route to Ethiopia; the disease outbreaks that almost wiped out the whole population in the camp; the hunger and the wild and angry creatures in the bush. We are all excited and happy to hear about you growing up well even though we are not there to support you. We think about you every day. Our advice is, no matter how young you are, just be a man. We know how strong you were when you were with us. Please keep up the same daily spirit.

We hade been told that the American government resettled you. Going to another country for safety reasons is not new to you anyway. Remember the day you all ran away from your village and the civil war in the country? America is a wonderful and peaceful country. You are going to be safe and secure there, compared to Kakuma Refugee camp where the hostile local population (Turkana) has killed some of you.

You are also going to be independent, not under the United Nation's care anymore. Make sure you go to school and work hard.

Another advice we are giving you is that some of our laws are comparatively different from the laws of the country where you are going to stay. Please respect the laws of the host country and you will not have problems at all. We also hear that the weather gets too cold around December. Make sure you dress up properly so you don't get sick. We don't want to hear that you have developed pneumonia.

Let us know when you are coming back to stay with us again. We have been told that you may come after a year or so. Best wishes from all of us. Stay strong, stay healthy and focus on your future. May Almighty God keep watch between you and us as we are away from one another.

We love you so much.

Ajak Mayen and Aluel Yuot.

EPILOGUE

Living without parents has taught me how difficult life is without their guidance. I survived war, disease and hunger with hope and determination, believing that one day God would bring peace to Sudan and that I would be reunited with my parents and siblings.

I didn't give up on myself. No matter how hard life was back then, I fought for my life, and remained optimistic, believing there were better days ahead of me. If you cannot fight for your life or do the right thing, then no one will help you out of your situation. You must stand up for yourself. That's what I did. I kept my faith and hope alive so that I could overcome the hardships of war and life in a refugee camp.

In life, you cannot stress yourself out over something you have no control over. When you know you are not doing anything wrong, just let it go and turn a new page for yourself. When we were being bombed by the government of Sudan because of our religion, I overcame the hardship of war, not because I was very strong, but because I was determined not give in to hopeless thoughts about the future.

I came back to the US in 2009 as a different person, full of joy and happiness. There's nothing like family. Visiting Sudan was a healing process, which helped me to put away the bad memories of war and what I went through in the refugee camps in Ethiopia and Kenya. What I learned from this journey is that life is not a one-way street, but it is many journeys full of joy, happiness and sadness.

Problems are part of life, so you have to come up with a strategy to deal with them. It is up to you to make your life better. Even when my body gave up on me, my heart kept telling me to keep walking and you will reach a better place. I listened to my heart, and if I had not, I would not be able to tell my story.

Hearing about the human tragedy in the Middle East and Africa where thousands of migrants are dying every week, reminds me how the government of Sudan bombed our villages and killed thousands of people in Sudan.

When I see thousands of Syrian refugees flee from Syria and cross into Europe, it reminds me about the borders that I crossed in my journey to a promise land. For them and others facing such adversity I know this:

You must have a positive *attitude*. Never give up hope. You must always believe that there will be a better day, a better place.

Be strong and show *fortitude*. Be determined and never give up. Even when my body gave up on me, my heart did not and I kept going.

And always be grateful to those who walk with you and help you. Never hesitate to show your *gratitude* to God Almighty who is there for you on every step of your journey.

———————

help us at:

www.southernsudanschools.org

Resources

1. Personal Memoirs: Panther Ajak Mayen

2. Shutterstock Royalty Free Images

Made in the USA
Coppell, TX
28 March 2021

52581343R10095